SEIZING THE NONVIOLENT MOMENTS

Seizing the
Nonviolent Moments

Reflections on the Spirituality of Nonviolence
Through the Lens of Scripture

BY

Nancy Small

FOREWORD BY

Mary Lou Kownacki, OSB

CASCADE *Books* · Eugene, Oregon

SEIZING THE NONVIOLENT MOMENTS
Reflections on the Spirituality of Nonviolence Through the Lens of Scripture

Cascade Books
An Imprint of Wipf and Stock Publishers
199 W. 8th Ave., Suite 3
Eugene, OR 97401

www.wipfandstock.com

ISBN 13: 978-1-62654-756-6

Cataloging-in-Publication data:

Small, Nancy.

Seizing the nonviolent moments : reflections on the spirituality of nonviolence through the lens of Scripture / Nancy Small.

xxii + 126 p.; 23 cm—Includes bibliographical references.

ISBN 13: 978-1-62654-756-6

1. Nonviolence—Religious aspects—Christianity. 2. Spiritual life. I. Title.

BT736.6 S80 2015

Manufactured in the USA.

Haiku Mind: 108 Poems to Cultivate and Open Your Heart, by Patricia Donegan, ©2008 by Patricia Donegan. Reprinted by arrangement with The Permissions Company, Inc., on behalf of Shambhala Publications Inc., Boston, MA. www.shambhala.com.

New Revised Standard Version Bible: Anglicized Edition, copyright 1989, 1995, Division of Christian Education of the National Council of the Churches of Christ in the United States of America. Used by permission. All rights reserved.

Pax Christi USA, *Peaceweavings*, Summer 2011, Washington, DC, www.paxchristiusa. org. Used with permission.

US Conference of Catholic Bishops, *Confronting a Culture of Violence: A Catholic Framework for Action*, Washington, DC: November, 1994. Used with permission.

The Inclusive Bible: The First Egalitarian Translation, Priests for Equality, Lanham, MD: Rowman and Littlefield, 2007. Used with permission.

For Carl, who believed in this book before a word was ever written and offered wise and heartfelt support every step of the way.

Table of Contents

Foreword

NONVIOLENCE DOES NOT GET the respect it deserves in Christian circles. In my own Catholic tradition, for example, the United States bishops issued a peace pastoral over thirty years ago, called *The Challenge of Peace*, in which they legitimized nonviolence as a genuine Christian option.

And yet little's been done in official church circles to promote nonviolence as an authentic means of social change and as the desired theological stance of those who follow Jesus.

So the promotion of nonviolence is left primarily to peacemakers like Nancy Small, who do not minimize or flinch from the horror of escalating violence in our time, but devote their lives to experimenting with nonviolence and articulating its truth.

Small's book is centered on "nonviolent moments"—ordinary, daily decisions that shape our lives. She writes, "Life is filled with nonviolent moments. We face them every day . . . and we must choose how to respond." What is a nonviolent moment? This haiku captures such a moment.

> I kill an ant . . .
> and realize my three children
> were watching[1]

If each of us kept a log of our days, for even a week, we'd probably be surprised at the number of times we get to decide on a violent or nonviolent response to an unexpected confrontation or situation. Waiting in a long supermarket line while another customer argues with the checkout clerk. Getting cut off in traffic. Being verbally attacked by someone. Trying to sleep while a mosquito buzzes in our ear. Squashing an ant walking on the kitchen table.

---

1. Kato, *Haiku Mind*.

Small's point is that choosing small acts of nonviolence is a spiritual practice that eventually shapes a nonviolent heart. And if it's done by many people together it builds a powerful force that can stop injustice and war. Small recalls that millions chose the nonviolent alternative prior to the 2003 invasion of Iraq and flooded the streets around the globe.

The response to that moment resulted in the "largest, global, simultaneous nonviolent campaign in history." The movement was massive enough to have the *New York Times* refer to it as one of "two superpowers on the planet." For a brief moment in time we had a visual of the potential power of nonviolence in changing structures.

There are few things I appreciate more than a creative, imaginative interpretation of a familiar Scripture. Each chapter of Small's book is grounded in a particular Scripture and it was rewarding to find many fresh insights into old stories. I was especially taken with her reflections on the multiplication of loaves and fishes, the woman taken in adultery, and the man possessed by multiple demons.

She uses the story of the multiplication of loaves and fishes, for example, as a lesson in personal empowerment and responsibility. She points out that when the disciples told Jesus that the people were hungry, he responded, "How many loaves have you? Go and see." In other words, rather than perform an immediate miracle, Jesus first empowered his disciples by inviting them to look into their own hearts and souls to satisfy the hunger of the crowds. In our own time, Small challenges, the people are hungry for food, peace, and an end to violence. Jesus' words remain: "How many loaves have you? Go and see." What graces, gifts, and skills do you and I have that will heal the hungers of the people?

Her treatment of forgiveness—a major component of nonviolence—is strong and realistic. She does not call for cheap or surface forgiveness. She quotes the Columbian priest Leonel Narvaez: "Forgiveness is not forgetting but rather remembering with different eyes." Nor does she sugarcoat the consequences of the nonviolent choice. The purpose of the cross, she asserts, is that it presented Jesus with a nonviolent moment: Jesus knew what he was up against and chose nonviolence. "When the forces against us cause our resolve to waiver," she writes, "it is the image of Jesus forging ahead faithful to nonviolence that inspires us to persevere."

Small brings to this book a solid theological background and decades of experience in local and national nonviolent campaigns and activism. She draws from her years as national coordinator of Pax Christi USA, the

Catholic peace movement, and from the many retreats and workshops she's led on nonviolence. Most importantly, we hear through her the voices of the poor whom she companioned throughout Latin America and in the heart of New York City.

Seizing the Nonviolent Moments is a humble and accessible approach to nonviolence, written with the mind-set that none of us is ever fully nonviolent; we are all in process. The discussion questions that follow each chapter open this book to multiple audiences—classrooms, parishes, intentional communities, and individuals seeking personal reflection.

In the end, it's peacemakers such as Nancy Small who are preparing Christians to embrace nonviolence as a constitutive element of the gospel. If the institutional church ever decides to promote the nonviolence of Jesus with the power that they mandate in areas of sexuality, a library of theological, spiritual, and strategic books written by the faithful nonviolent remnant will be available. One of the first that church authorities should reach for is *Seizing the Nonviolent Moments.*

Mary Lou Kownacki, OSB

Sr. Mary Lou is Director of Benetvision Publishing in Erie, PA, and the online monastery Monasteries of the Heart. She is a former national coordinator of Pax Christi USA.

Acknowledgements

Many hands have helped to bring this book into being. I am grateful to all who have inspired and supported me in the years that this book has been taking shape, a list too long to include in its entirety. I wish to mention especially:

- Pax Christi, the international Catholic movement for peace, where the seeds of my spirituality of nonviolence were planted and grew. Thank you, Pax Christi, for encouraging me to write about the spirituality of nonviolence long ago and for affirming so much of what I have written over the years.

- My mentors in the ways of Ignatian spirituality, including many Jesuits, the Jesuit Volunteer Corps, and retreat directors throughout the years. They have given me resources to dive beneath the surface of Scripture to discover the wisdom waiting to be found in the deepening places.

- The Benedictine community of Erie, sisters and oblates, for their faithfulness to the works of mercy, the works of justice, and the works of peace. Special thanks to Mary Lou Kownacki, OSB, for inspiring me with her writings and blessing this book with its foreword.

- Kim McElaney, in memoriam, who called forth the spiritual writer in me through her steadfast belief in my vocation.

- The many friends and colleagues who have read portions of this book and offered me feedback, especially Chris Schweitzer, whose insights helped me bring the book's content into its final form.

- Peacemakers who have hosted and attended workshops, conferences, and retreats where I have presented material from this book as it was being developed. Their clarity, confusion, enthusiasm, insights, and ennui helped me to see which sections were complete and which needed more work.

- Spiritual directors and guides who kindled sparks of hope in my doubt, especially Janet Ruffing, RSM, Marie Therese Martin, CSJ, Katie Kelly, and Nicki Verploegen.

- My circle of friends and family who offered ongoing encouragement over the years and excitement in the final stages of writing, most especially Carl for being the voice of gentle persistence.

- Rosemarie Pace, whose title for a Pax Christi Metro New York retreat that I led became the title for this book.

- Rodney Clapp at Wipf and Stock, for guiding me through the wilderness of formatting and editing my manuscript, and all those at Cascade Books who helped at every stage of the book's publication.

Abbreviations

Cor	Corinthians
Deut	Deuteronomy
Eph	Ephesians
Exod	Exodus
Gen	Genesis
Isa	Isaiah
Lev	Leviticus
Matt	Matthew
NRSV	*New Revised Standard Version Bible: Anglicized Edition*
TIB	*The Inclusive Bible: The First Egalitarian Translation*
TRC	Truth and Reconciliation Commission

Introduction

WHEN I FIRST BECAME aware of the call of nonviolence in my life, I was like a sponge. I read as much as I could. I learned from people who had been walking the way of nonviolence for many years. I attended talks on peacemaking and participated in nonviolent vigils and demonstrations. I read daily reflections on nonviolence and contemplated their meaning in my life. I beseeched God to lead me on this journey I had begun and help me make sense of it all. It was as if a fire had been kindled in me that set my soul to burning. The more I stoked the flames of this fire through my exploration of nonviolence, the stronger it blazed within me.

Like most of the calls I've received in my life, this one came with a fair amount of wrestling. I was a seminary student at the time. I had the great privilege of studying liberation theology with students from countries engaged in liberation struggles. Some of these students advocated nonviolence while others strongly defended the rights of oppressed peoples to engage in armed struggles for independence. My fellow students often reminded me that as an American I knew nothing of the suffering of oppressed peoples throughout the world. They cautioned me about advocating nonviolence from my lofty place of privilege and power as a citizen of a First World nation.

I wrestled with these voices and my own inner voice. I wrestled in prayer with what felt like a deepening call to embrace the way of nonviolence. And I remembered my visit several years earlier to war-torn El Salvador, a nation engaged in its own liberation struggle at that time. During my visit, I looked into the frightened eyes of young Salvadoran soldiers who were wearing US army uniforms and whose fighting was funded by US tax dollars. I looked into the anguished eyes of impoverished people whose lives were torn apart by the war. Evidence of the pain and destruction wrought by the violence was everywhere. Of course it mattered whether the bullets and bombs came from the government army or from those fighting against them for liberation. But the blood-soaked streets and shattered lives looked the same, regardless of who was responsible.

My wrestling eventually led me to embrace the way of nonviolence. Over the years, I've read many inspirational and influential writings. But none has been more important in my own formation than a groundbreaking essay written by Mary Lou Kownacki, OSB. Sr. Mary Lou went beyond the practice of nonviolence to write about the spirituality that enlivens it. Reflecting on a passage in St. Paul's Letter to the Ephesians, Sr. Mary Lou writes, "A spirituality of nonviolence has something to do with grasping fully the depth and height and length and breadth of Christ's love, experiencing it, and making it visible."[1] This definition of a spirituality rooted in Christian faith spoke strongly to my experience.

Years later, I discovered another essay that furthered my understanding of this love that we are called to make visible. I found the essay in a book exploring the prophet Micah's command to act justly, love tenderly, and walk humbly with God. Writing about the command to love tenderly, Sharon Parks quotes Scripture scholar Paul Hanson's belief that "the love referred to here is . . . like Yahweh's covenant love . . . it is a love that reaches out to us not only tenderly but also tenaciously."[2] These two dimensions of God's love spoke to my experience of how we are to make Christ's love visible in a multidimensional world.

The spirituality of nonviolence is fueled by a love that is both tender and tenacious. This love reaches out with great tenderness when it recognizes the fragility of life and the need to be gentle. It reaches out with great tenacity when it stands up with daring and determination wherever life is threatened. The spirituality of nonviolence is rooted in a love that invites clenched hearts and hands to open by gently touching them with patience, kindness, and mercy. It is also rooted in a love that seeks to disarm individuals and dismantle systems of injustice by boldly speaking its truth.

This tender and tenacious love burned strong in the heart of Jesus. When we think of his life, we are often drawn to the tender acts of love that characterized his ministry. Again and again, Jesus reached out to individuals and groups with compassion and mercy. He melted the sting of injustice by blessing peacemakers and those persecuted for the sake of righteousness. He looked upon those who were oppressed with the loving

1. Kownacki, *Love Beyond Measure*, 3.
2. Brueggemann et al., *To Act Justly, Love Tenderly, Walk Humbly*, 39.

gaze of God, letting them know they were precious in God's eyes. He affirmed God's great love for the poor and marginalized each time he cast in those who society cast out. He invited hearts of stone to become hearts of flesh by offering forgiveness again and again and again.

Just as important as the ways Jesus loved tenderly are the ways he loved tenaciously. We see this prophetic love at work each time Jesus challenged the law of the land with the law of God's love. He countered "an eye for an eye" thinking by commanding his followers to turn the other cheek to evildoers and go the extra mile for them. He spoke truth to power by publicly chastising the civil and religious authorities for their misdeeds. Jesus refused to be coerced or co-opted by those who opposed him and remained firmly committed to his mission. The tenacious love he put into practice was strong enough to stir the soul of society and threaten the rulers of his day.

Jesus lived this tender and tenacious love moment by moment, person by person. When opportunities to put this love into action came his way, he seized them. When they didn't, he created them. Jesus lived the spirituality of nonviolence, and he called his followers to live it as well. His ministry did not melt every chain of injustice or every shackle of oppression binding society. Jesus was crucified long before he was able to achieve the full transformation of the world. Yet he seized every nonviolent moment he could, leaving us lessons to follow and a legacy to uphold.

To embrace a spirituality of nonviolence is to follow in the footsteps of Jesus and other leaders in the nonviolent tradition. These leaders include those ancestors in faith who model nonviolence through the stories of Scripture. They include leaders in more recent history whose names are well known to us, including those who were martyred for upholding the nonviolent way. They include as well those whose names are unknown to us, countless numbers of people who have strengthened the way of nonviolence by giving themselves to it. And they include those of us baptized into the Christian faith, for through our baptism we have been given nonviolence as our blessing and our birthright.

The way of nonviolence doesn't come naturally to many of us. It's not something most of us learned in religious education classes. Most programs of faith formation don't delve deeply into the spirituality of nonviolence. In fact, many of them never mention it at all. So we need to fill in the gaps that exist in our formation. We need to understand what nonviolence is and what it isn't. We need to explore the spirituality that enlivens it. And we need to build a spiritual foundation within ourselves that will strengthen and support us as we follow the way of nonviolence.

This book is my contribution to your formation in the spirituality of nonviolence. It was Scripture that first gave me an understanding of the spirituality of nonviolence, and over the years it has given me great spiritual support. I delved deeply into it during my seminary days and fell in love with it so much that it has become a vital part of my own spirituality. Scripture instructs and inspires me and gives words to my lament when the world's turmoil overwhelms me. It offers me the spiritual sustenance I need to keep going. And it is through the wisdom of Scripture that I have learned profound truths about the spirituality of nonviolence.

Each chapter of this book is rooted in Scripture and many chapters weave in stories of people and places that have formed me along the way. The Scripture passages I've selected are those I've reflected upon over the years and used in workshops and talks. Yet the ten chapters of this book barely begin to tap into all the nonviolent wisdom that Scripture holds. So I approach this book as a humble attempt to glean an iota of the great wisdom Scripture has to offer us in the spirituality of nonviolence.

Scripture quotations are taken from the *New Revised Standard Version Bible* (NRSV) as well as *The Inclusive Bible: The First Egalitarian Translation* (TIB). The NRSV is the version of scripture that I have studied and prayed with for many years and so it is close to my heart. I turn to TIB when its translation offers more inclusive language while maintaining the meaning of the text as it appears in the NRSV. My efforts to use inclusive language remind me that human language will always be limited as it attempts to capture the immensity of God. As you read, I invite you to use whatever language draws you closer to God and invites you into the Scripture passages. If you encounter language that feels confining, open it up by substituting words that connect you with your image of the divine.

Most chapters of this book draw upon the wisdom of the US Catholic bishops' 1994 pastoral message *Confronting a Culture of Violence*. The bishops issued this message in response to what they perceived to be a growing culture of violence. In the twenty years since it was written, the wisdom contained in this message has become more true, not less. Life has changed a great deal since the events of September 11, 2001, and the need to confront a growing culture of violence is great. It is my hope that this book will shed new light upon the insights this pastoral message contains as we seek to transform our troubled times.

Some of you reading this book have been opening yourselves up to nonviolence for quite some time. Others began by opening this book. Wherever you may find yourself, the important thing is to remain open. Pay attention to the stirrings of nonviolence within you. Open yourself up to the vast truths that it longs to teach you. Remember, too, that each of us is a work in progress. The ways we practice nonviolence won't be perfect. But if we continue to grow in our understanding of nonviolence, we will grow in our lived expression of it. And we will be inspired by those who are much further along in their journey than we are. Much is asked of those who open themselves up to the way of nonviolence. But even more is offered.

In August of 1995, I was named acting national coordinator of Pax Christi USA, the Catholic movement for peace. The following November, the national council offered me the position of national coordinator during its fall meeting. I humbly accepted their offer by removing my shoes. I read one of my favorite quotes, which happened to be the quote for that day in a booklet entitled *Peacemaking Day by Day.* "Our first task in approaching another people, another culture, another religion," writes Max Warren, "is to take off our shoes, for the place we are approaching is holy. Else we may find ourselves treading on people's dreams. More serious still, we may forget that God was here before our arrival."[3]

As we approach the spirituality of nonviolence together, I take off my shoes and I invite you to do the same, for the place we are approaching is holy. We are approaching a way of life that beckons us toward the holy ground of our hearts in a spirit of honesty and humility. We are approaching a love strong enough to break down walls of hatred and hostility. We are walking a path pioneered by holy women and men who have given themselves heart and soul for the sake of a peaceful future. We are tapping into the holy ground of our being in order to discover the transformative power of nonviolence that lies deep within.

As we journey let us remember that God was here long before our arrival. God is with us as we wrestle with the call and the challenge of nonviolence. And God will be here beckoning others to this holy ground long after our traveling days are done.

3. Pax Christi USA, *Peacemaking Day by Day,* 136.

1

Seizing the Nonviolent Moments

LIFE IS FILLED WITH nonviolent moments. We face them every day. Sometimes these moments come upon us suddenly, as when a conflict arises unexpectedly and we must decide how to respond. Can I find a way to be helpful rather than hurtful in a conflict that involves me directly? Will I offer forgiveness to someone who has done me wrong? Can I help guide others mired in conflict toward reconciliation? Other nonviolent moments are not nearly as obvious, like those that have to do with the way we live our lives. Does my way of life reduce or enlarge my carbon footprint? Do I speak out against social injustice or remain silent? Do I make a conscious effort to purchase from companies that employ just labor practices while avoiding those that don't?

These are just a few examples of the many nonviolent moments we face as individuals. Others arise in the context of our identity as people integrally linked to one another in the web of life. How will a community respond to heightened gang activity and a rising crime rate? Will a nation use military or diplomatic means to respond to a perceived threat? Do community leaders enact policies that help those who are poor and marginalized or push them further into the margins? Will global leaders work in ways that promote unity and understanding among nations, or mistrust and fear?

Nonviolent moments call us to make a choice. We seize these moments when we choose to act in a spirit of nonviolence. We squander them when we don't.

Seizing the nonviolent moments is about taking hold of the opportunities we have to practice the way of nonviolence. Yet sometimes these opportunities don't look like opportunities at all. This is especially true when we find ourselves caught up in the throes of a conflict or facing an unjust situation where we feel like the cards are stacked against us. As unwelcome as these moments can be, they present occasions for us to further the reach of nonviolence in our world.

When I think about what it means to seize the nonviolent moments, I think about the Scripture story of God first forming creation. This great story brings the passion of God to contend with the power of chaos. "In the beginning when God created the heavens and the earth," begins the book of Genesis, "the earth was a formless void, and darkness covered the face of the deep, while a wind from God swept over the face of the waters" (Gen 1:1–2, NRSV). We imagine this embryonic earth as a place of chaos. But to God it was so much more. It was a dark and watery womb filled with all kinds of possibilities for what it might become. What was needed was the touch of transformation. God reached into the chaos with the power of a generative love, giving birth to creation in all its beauty.

In this Scripture story, God faced a nonviolent moment. God could choose to do nothing and allow chaos to reign. Or he could engage the chaos with creativity and compassion. God could allow darkness to continue blanketing the face of the earth. Or she could reach into this hollow place with her hallowed touch to make of it something more. God made a compelling choice for life and love, believing that out of the chaos something good could emerge. And so it did.

We face a similar challenge today, for God knows there is no shortage of chaos in these troubled times. In their 1994 pastoral message *Confronting a Culture of Violence*, the US Catholic Bishops wrote:

> Violence—in our homes, our schools and streets, our nation and world—is destroying the lives, dignity and hopes of millions of sisters and brothers. Fear of violence is paralyzing and polarizing our communities . . .
>
> Hostility, hatred, despair and indifference are at the heart of a growing culture of violence. . . . Our social fabric is being torn apart by a culture of violence that leaves children dead in our streets and families afraid in our homes. . . . A nation born in a commitment to "life, liberty and the pursuit of happiness" is

haunted by death, imprisoned by fear and caught up in the elusive pursuit of protection rather than happiness.[1]

This sobering social analysis rings even more true today. We are indeed a nation imprisoned by fear and caught up in the elusive pursuit of protection. Our nation pours hundreds of billions of dollars each year into our bloated military budget to protect our borders from imagined attacks while cash-starved states slash their budgets for the very real needs of education, jobs, and affordable housing. Wars and military campaigns waged since September 11, 2001 have created new enemies and deepening enmity. Our streets and schools have become less safe, not more, as gun violence has grown. In less than a year's time we've experienced the killing of Trayvon Martin, the movie massacre in Colorado, and the school shooting in Newtown, Connecticut. The vitriol expressed by groups of disgruntled people and politicians throughout our country is placing a choke hold on civility. And waging war has become a way of life for our nation.

These are just a few examples of the chaos that is plunging our nation into a deepening state of despair. We are charting a course that is leading toward our spiritual and social demise. Not only is the chaos evident all around us. It is evident within us as well, manifesting itself in any number of unsettling ways. It is our angst over the present state of the world and the sense of foreboding we feel when we ponder its future. It is the heartache that grows each time we hear about lives being carelessly tossed around and callously disregarded in society. It is the bewilderment that overcomes us and the sense of not knowing what to do about it all that rattles in the recesses of our souls.

More than forty-five years ago, the Rev. Martin Luther King Jr. sensed the direction we were headed and issued a stark warning. "We still have a choice today: nonviolent coexistence or violent coannihilation," he said. "This may well be mankind's last chance to choose between chaos and community."[2]

God faced a choice about whether or not to contend with chaos. And so do we. We can choose to do nothing and allow chaos to reign. We can throw up our hands believing there is little or nothing we can do to transform these troubled times. Or we can choose to answer the prophetic call of Rev. King by following the example God gave us.

1. US Conference of Catholic Bishops, *Confronting a Culture of Violence*, Section I, "Introduction."

2. Washington, ed., *The Essential Writings and Speeches*, 633.

When we seize the nonviolent moments of our lives, we are choosing to contend with chaos. We are rejecting the ways of violence that cause suffering and injustice. We are choosing instead to bring the power of nonviolence to bear upon the problems we face. And we are contributing to the creation of a global community that works cooperatively for the well-being of all.

Nonviolence is a force that seeks not to harm but to heal, not to break down but to build up. It seeks to transfigure our world without trouncing opposing forces. It reaches beyond confusion and chaos toward answers that seem to lie far beyond our understanding. It transcends love limited by myriad conditions toward a love that knows no bounds. The spirituality of nonviolence erases lines drawn in the sand and traces the contours of common ground. It refuses to give into despair because it is alive with the breath of hope. Each nonviolent action we take leaves its imprint and invites others to follow in our footsteps. Little by little, we build the foundation of a world at peace from the firmament of a world constrained by chaos.

There is great wisdom in the way God contended with chaos. The Genesis story speaks of creation being fashioned one day at a time. God plunged into the chaos and brought forth creation step by beautiful step. The Holy One focused on what was needed, day by day, until at last the work of creation was finished. Each day that God engaged the chaos mattered in the context of the whole of creation. What was brought forth one day set the stage for what would be brought forth the next. At the end of most days, God reflected on what was created and "saw that it was good" (Gen 1:12b, NRSV). In God's good time, the act of creation utterly transformed the chaos.

God labored day by day and step by step. Twenty years ago, the US bishops called people of faith to do the same when contending with chaos. "Violence is overcome day by day, choice by choice, person by person," they wrote in their pastoral message. "All of us must make a contribution."[3]

This is precisely how we are called to transform the violence of our times. We do this day by day, believing that what we do today sets the stage for what will come tomorrow. We seize these moments in our lives one by one even when they seem small or insignificant. Each one is just as important as the next, just as each part of creation was important to God. And

---

3. US Conference of Catholics Bishops, *Confronting a Culture of Violence*, Section IV, "A Framework for Action."

when God gazes upon our efforts to transform the chaos, God sees that it is very good.

The bishops make it clear that none of us are exempt from this transformative work. All of us can and must contribute. No matter how much turmoil or trouble we may face, the invitation is one and the same. We are not to remain idle and allow chaos to reign. We are not to turn away from the chance to choose nonviolence. We are to reach into the chaos, cocreating with God to make of these moments what we can.

I love the description of the earth as a formless void before God intervened to form creation. Why? Because a void is a great big opening. And in every opening lies potential. Within every nonviolent moment, no matter how difficult or daunting, there is an opening. In every chaotic situation lies a hidden opportunity. These openings may not be spacious and obvious. They may be small and hard to find. But they are there, waiting to be discovered.

These openings can be found in the uneasy quiet that follows a contentious conflict. They are the pregnant pause we face whenever we must choose between doing what is right or what is wrong. They are the open wounds of society created by war, injustice, and every form of violence. These openings invite us to enter in. They are the fertile places where we can engage the chaos with the creativity of nonviolence in an effort to repair the fabric of our tattered world.

I'd like to share a story that offers a powerful example of how these openings in the midst of chaos can become entryways for nonviolence. Years ago, the Benedictine Sisters of Erie, Pennsylvania began a custom of inviting people to gather in prayer each time someone was murdered in their city. They went to the place where the murder happened. A flyer announcing one of these prayer vigils described the spirit of their gathering in this way. "We need to reclaim the place where violence has occurred. We need to pray for all people who are victims of violence. We need to believe that a nonviolent way of life is possible."

Within the chaos and calamity of murder, these sisters saw an opening. The murder created a wound within their community. But they understood that it also created a space to bring the grace of nonviolence to a place greatly in need of healing. I remember the power that I experienced each time I attended one of these prayer vigils during my years in Erie. We were a group of people seizing the nonviolent moment together. We were bringing the power of prayer to a place of pain. We prayed for the person who died and their loved ones. We prayed for those responsible for the murder and their loved ones. We prayed for all the innocent victims of violence. And we prayed for the way of nonviolence to somehow take hold in the wake of this tragedy.

This is what seizing the nonviolent moment is all about. It's about choosing to stop the hemorrhaging in our world and start the healing. It's about looking beyond the pain caused by a harmful act toward reconciliation. We reclaim the places in our personal lives that have been strained or broken by violence. We reclaim the places in society harmed by individual incidents of violence as well as those harmed by systemic violence. In this way, we proclaim our belief that a nonviolent way of life is truly possible. And we claim our responsibility to do our part in bringing it about.

Reaching into these openings with the touch of nonviolence can sometimes have a far-reaching effect. Prophet and peacemaker Dorothy Day once wrote, "What we would like to do is change the world—make it a little simpler for people to feed, clothe and shelter themselves as God intended them to do. . . . [W]e can to a certain extent change the world; we can work for the oasis, the little cell of joy and peace in a harried world. We can throw our pebble in the pond and be confident that its ever-widening circle will reach around the world."[4]

Nonviolent moments have a lot to do with how we throw our pebbles in the ponds of our lives. They call us to make a conscious choice by thinking about the ripple effects our actions have on others. As Dorothy suggests, these ripples create an ever-widening circle that can be far-reaching. And so we must choose carefully. What kind of ripples do we want to send out to those who form the circles of our lives? And what kind of ripples do we wish to send round the world? We can create ripples that reach out to touch others with compassion and healing. Or we can create ripples that cause harm in some way to our sisters and brothers, both near and far.

The choice is ours to make, day to day and moment to moment. This means that even when we throw our pebbles in ways we later regret, we can always choose differently the next time. And we can learn from those whose peaceful ripples are reaching out in ways we seek to follow.

I remember a time years ago when I was leading a workshop on peacemaking. I don't remember much about the specifics of the workshop, but I remember very clearly a nonviolent moment I faced during the midst of it. Sadly, I squandered the moment. But a veteran peacemaker in the group

4. Ellsberg, ed., *By Little and By Little*, 98.

named Art seized it. His actions transformed the situation and taught me an important lesson in the process.

Early on in the workshop, I became aware of a man who seemed restless and disquieting. He was quick to challenge the content of my presentation. He spoke out of turn and dominated conversation. The nonviolent moment arrived when something provoked him and he became especially loud and disruptive. I was unnerved by his behavior, and I began to react defensively, raising my voice in turn. If I didn't do something to control the situation, I thought, things could very quickly get out of hand.

As I began raising my voice, Art quietly spoke up. Out of respect for him, I stopped talking and gave him the floor. Not knowing the man's name, he said softly, "My brother." He repeated these two words ever so gently until the man stopped yelling and looked directly at him. Art then connected with the man on a deeper level. Through a series of questions, he was able to get an idea of what was bothering this man. He conveyed empathy and understanding. The troubled man responded to Art's nonviolent intervention and became still. He was disarmed of his anger, and he stopped being disruptive for the remainder of the workshop.

This seasoned peacemaker seized the nonviolent moment with compassion and creativity. He calmed a contentious encounter and skillfully found a way to transform the situation. He carved out a safe space for the man to let down his guard, and he made himself vulnerable in the process. He threw a gentle pebble into the pond of that classroom, and its ripples reached out to touch not only the man but the entire group of people who were there. I have no doubt that those who came to the workshop were touched by that transformative moment much more than they were touched by anything I said that day.

Seizing the nonviolent moment can be as simple as taking time to listen to a person's pain, as it was in this example, and disarming the person's anger in the process. Or it can be as challenging as choosing nonviolence day after day in the personal and public decisions we make.

Some of the nonviolent moments we face are much more inconspicuous than the one described above. Let's take for example the decision about whether or not to drink bottled water, a choice many of us have probably faced. On the surface, this doesn't appear to be a choice between helping or harming others. It doesn't seem to have anything to do with violence or injustice. It looks like a simple choice based on personal preference or need.

But when we learn more about the bottled water industry, we begin to see the harmful effects it has on others.

Thirsty Americans drink more bottled water than any other nation. When we choose bottled water, we contribute to a global system of corporate-owned water. As more water sources are owned by private corporations, fewer remain available for public consumption. This is a growing problem because it is expected that two-thirds of the world population will run short of drinking water by 2025. Another factor to consider is that more than 1.5 million barrels of oil are required each year to produce enough plastic bottles to satisfy Americans' demand for bottled water. Lastly, if we do not recycle our plastic bottles, we are contributing to the two million tons of discarded water bottles clogging landfills.[5]

Like Dorothy Day said, our actions have a ripple effect, as this example clearly indicates. Which is why it's so important to seize these moments in the way we live our personal lives. When we refrain from drinking bottled water, we remove ourselves from a system that causes harm to people and the planet. In this way, we send out a tiny ripple of healing. This choice may involve some sacrifice on our part, like remembering to carry a refillable water bottle and finding places to fill it. But this is a small sacrifice to make in order to stop being part of the problem and instead become part of the solution.

I once met with a group of students who were eager to hear more about the way of nonviolence. I shared these statistics about the growing bottled water industry with them and later learned that a group of students had already begun educating themselves about this issue and organizing for action. They began educating others on their campus. They encouraged the use of refillable water bottles and sold them at various gatherings. Finally, they entered into dialogue with top college officials, advocating that bottled water be eliminated from campus activities that offered beverages.

The results? More and more people began using refillable water bottles. And eventually the students secured a commitment from college officials to eliminate bottled water from their beverage service.

These students show us that the nonviolent ripples we send out can lead to real change in our communities. They can also lead to real change in our souls, for these ripples reach not only outward but inward as well.

The spirituality of nonviolence washes over our souls like moving water washes over stones immersed in it. The more we immerse ourselves in

5. The Water Project, Inc., *Why Water?*

8

this spirituality, the more we are shaped by the ebb and flow of nonviolence upon us. The hardened places in us slowly begin to soften. The rough edges of our souls gradually grow smoother. The more we seize the nonviolent moments, the more we are transformed by them. Each of us is an ongoing act of creation, formed and fashioned as we give ourselves to the way of nonviolence. We grow as the ripples touch more and more layers of who we are. The more we experience the power of nonviolence within ourselves, the more we come to believe in the potential it holds for our world.

In the Genesis creation story, Scripture tells us that above the deep and dark abyss "a wind from God swept over the face of the waters" (Gen 1:2, NRSV). When wind sweeps across a body of water, it stirs it up. When we give ourselves to nonviolence, it stirs us up. It stirs in us a passion for peace. It stirs up our living with nonviolent loving. It stirs up a determination to join with others to make of our battered world a better world.

When we join with others in this work, the spirit of nonviolence begins to stir the soul of society. Those who discover the promise that nonviolence holds for our world are stirred into action. Individuals fed up with oppression move from standing on the sidelines to standing up for what they believe. As more and more people come together, the nonviolent ripples we create turn into waves. Out of the nonviolent moment emerges a nonviolent movement stirring the soul of society with steadfast determination. We become like the potent wind of God blowing through our world, countering the chaos with the passion and power of nonviolence.

I remember a day years ago when our world felt the power of this wind blowing as never before. It was February, 2003 and our nation was readying itself to invade Iraq. National leaders were claiming that Iraq was actively seeking to produce nuclear weapons. We were told that al-Qaida was harboring terrorists there. As our national leaders built their case for war, the US military was preparing itself to bombard Iraq as never before. And the international peace movement was organizing itself to protest as never before.

On February 15, 2003, people across the globe rose up in nation after nation. On this day millions of people seized the nonviolent moment by participating in coordinated peaceful demonstrations around the world. Many of these people engaged in nonviolent action for the first time that day. People who never imagined themselves taking to the streets. People who never considered themselves political. People who never considered seizing the nonviolent moment until that moment. People of many races and economic classes, people from the labor movement, the peace movement, and the antiglobalization movement, stirred up our world as never before with the mighty wind of nonviolent transformation.

On that day we glimpsed what is possible when people around the globe seize the nonviolent moment and together generate a surging tide of transformation. Throngs of people joined together to stop the war and created waves of change. This was the largest, global, simultaneous nonviolent campaign in history, a show of force so strong that even the media couldn't ignore it. An article in the *New York Times* two days later referred to this worldwide public outcry as one of "two superpowers on the planet,"[6] with the United States being the other. It was truly a watershed moment for nonviolence.

Some will say that this outpouring of nonviolent action failed to achieve its purpose since it did not succeed in stopping the Iraq War. What was most important about that day, however, was not what it accomplished but what it began. On that day, extraordinary numbers of people around the world renounced violence and embraced nonviolence. Crowds of people greater than anyone imagined poured into the streets. Nation after nation came together in a global outcry against war. And nonviolence spoke with a voice heard round the world. Leaders of nations interrupted business as usual and took notice. People around the world interrupted daily life and took notice. And the millions of people marching in the streets put the world on notice, demonstrating without a doubt that nonviolence is a global force to be reckoned with.

On that day we did indeed glimpse the budding of a second superpower, a superpower that is stirring as never before. It is stirring in the womb of our world, cultivating nonviolent beginnings where violence and injustice have long reigned. It is stirring with courage and conviction in the souls of more and more people. It is a superpower alive with the promise of what it can accomplish, striving to realize its full potential. As scholar Jonathan Schell has written, "The cooperative power of nonviolent action . . . has already altered basic realities that everyone must work with. . . . In the century ahead, it can be our bulwark and shield against the still unmastered peril of total violence."[7]

We have the power to make nonviolence into this bulwark and shield. We can find the openings in our world and engage them with nonviolence.

6. Patrick E. Tyler, "A New Power In the Streets," *New York Times*, February 17, 2003.

7. Schell, "The Unconquerable World," 431.

We can cast our nonviolent pebbles into the global pond and experience their ripples racing outward. Together we can be the strong wind stirring up tidal waves of transformation to touch the most turbulent parts of our world. Nonviolence has the potential to bridge the wide expanse between the world God loved into being and the world generation after generation has bruised into brokenness. It is the only reconciling force known to our world with the power to lead us from global chaos to global community.

The choice is ours. And the future of our world depends upon it.

Questions for Reflection and Conversation

1. What does it mean to you to "seize the nonviolent moment?"

2. The Rev. Martin Luther King Jr. said that society has a choice between chaos and community. Do you agree? In what ways is our society choosing chaos? In what ways is it choosing community?

3. Can you think of a time when you seized a nonviolent moment? What happened? Can you think of a time when you squandered a nonviolent moment? What might you have done differently?

4. How do you throw your pebble into the global pond through your daily living? What kind of ripples do you wish to send out and what changes might be needed in your life to do this?

5. Where is the touch of nonviolence needed within you? Are there parts of you that are in need of softening or rough edges needing to be smoothed?

6. Do you believe that nonviolence can become a second superpower strong enough to significantly change the future of our world? Why/ why not? What will it take for nonviolence to become this kind of superpower?

2

Bringing What We Have to the Table

WHEN I THINK ABOUT the spirituality of nonviolence, I think of abundance. Nonviolence is an abundantly powerful force capable of countering the violence that overshadows our world. Yet many people associate nonviolence not with abundance but with absence. Some mistakenly believe nonviolence is merely the absence of violence. Others believe it is passive or weak. They assume that nonviolence has little or nothing to offer in the face of violence, as if it were a nonresponse. Still others assume that it could never muster enough strength to pose a serious challenge to the levels of violence that increasingly plague our world. Even those of us who believe in the power of nonviolence sometimes doubt if it can really be effective when we face a particularly challenging situation.

Despite these misperceptions and doubts, nonviolence has proven itself again and again as a force abundantly able to confront violence. The word *nonviolence* may be a noun, but it always behaves like a verb. It knows how to be patient, but it is never passive. It is filled with a spirit that does not give in, give over, or give up. This spirit does not lose heart, especially when the chips are down. For it is when the chips are down that the nonviolent moment opens wide with possibility, inviting a nonviolent response.

When I reflect on the abundance of nonviolence, my heart finds its way to the familiar Gospel account of Jesus multiplying the loaves and fishes. In this amazing story, a hungry crowd is fed with just five loaves of bread and a couple of fish. This miracle is the only one recorded in all four Gospels, which suggests something about its importance. Scripture tells us more than 5,000 people ate that day and still there was enough extra food to fill twelve baskets (see Mark 6:43). It's clearly a miracle about absence being transformed into abundance. And the type of power present in this miracle bears a strong resemblance to the power of nonviolence.

In the synoptic Gospels, this miracle takes place just after the gruesome beheading of John the Baptist. If this tragic event weren't awful enough we also learn that Herod, who ordered the death of John, has begun to keep a wary eye upon Jesus (see Mark 6:14–16). John's death must have been devastating for Jesus, and the awareness of Herod's scrutiny only intensified the uncertainty of that difficult time. It's easy to imagine questions creeping into his consciousness. What would the future hold for him now that John had been killed? Would his fate be the same? With Herod's attention turned toward Jesus, he had good reason to be concerned.

With all of this as a backdrop Jesus finds himself standing before a hungry crowd, considering how to respond. The choice he faces isn't simply about feeding the crowd or sending it away hungry. There's something much greater at stake for him. He can choose to continue on in his ministry undeterred by Herod's scrutiny. Or he can choose to tone down his actions for awhile in the hope that Herod might turn his attention away from him. Jesus is faced with a choice about who he is and how he will act with the eyes of the people and the powers that be upon him.

The choice of Jesus is what we might expect. He responds in faithfulness to the needs of the crowd before him without counting the personal cost involved. He risks his own well-being for the sake of his ministry and mission. Rather than lying low for a bit, he seizes the nonviolent moment by orchestrating his largest miracle, one that is broad in scope and bold in significance. And he does so in a way that emboldens and empowers his followers as never before.

Jesus demonstrates staunch determination in a time of doubt. He shows the disciples and the crowd that he will not shrink down or give in when faced with a challenge. Instead, he will become more, not less. He shows those who have come to him that they are not to cower before the death-dealing powers. Like Jesus, they are to reach into the nonviolent moment and make of it what they can. They are to be the leaven of love that reaches out and touches those in need. They are to be the bread of nonviolence broken and shared in a society hungering for liberation.

In order to see how this miracle relates more fully to the spirituality of nonviolence, we must look closely at the way Jesus carries it out. Here

I invite us to turn our attention to Mark's Gospel, which offers the most detailed account of what took place.

Scripture tells us that Jesus has been teaching a large crowd for a good part of the day. The hour is drawing late, and the people are hungry. The disciples suggest dispersing the crowd so the people can go to the villages to find food. But Jesus has something else in mind. He tells the disciples, "You give them something to eat" (Mark 6:37a, NRSV). The disciples don't understand what Jesus means, so they ask, "Are we to go and buy two hundred denarii worth of bread, and give it to them to eat?" (Mark 6:37b, NRSV). They know they haven't brought nearly enough food for everyone and they cannot fathom spending that kind of money.

We could simply view the response of Jesus as one of those times when he seems reluctant to intervene, like when he tells Mary his hour hasn't come at the wedding feast at Cana. But in this case I think Jesus responds as he does for a very specific reason. In the aftermath of John the Baptist's death, it's becoming increasingly clear that the future doesn't bode well for him. Jesus needs to prepare for the day when he will no longer be with his disciples. The time has come for Jesus to challenge them to rely less on him and more on themselves.

Jesus asks his disciples, "How many loaves have you? Go and see" (Mark 6:38, NRSV). The answer doesn't lie beyond you, Jesus suggests. The answer lies among you and within you. There's no need to rush off to the marketplace. Each of you must look within yourself to see what you can bring to the table. All of you must consider what you have to give collectively as a community. Go, see what you have to offer, and bring it to me.

When the disciples take these words to heart, they do not come up empty. They find among themselves five loaves of bread and two fish. They bring this food to Jesus and wait to see what he will do.

Jesus then tells the disciples to have the people sit down in groups. "So they sat down in groups of hundreds and of fifties," Scripture tells us (Mark 6:40, NRSV). It's as if Jesus has suddenly become a community organizer! And for good reason. He's organizing the crowd in order to carry out the plan he has in mind. The first step is to get them to sit down so that everyone can see him. Once the people are seated, Jesus lifts the bread, blesses it, breaks it, and gives it "to his disciples to set before the people" (Mark 6:41, NRSV). Jesus offers an example to all who are gathered and waits to see what will happen.

We'll never know exactly how everyone received enough food that day. All of the Gospels omit these very important details, leaving plenty of room for us to explore what might have happened. We are invited into the text to imagine what took place after the disciples set the loaves before the people. We are invited to imagine how we would have entered into the experience if we were there. And we are invited to feel the power that flowed through the feeding of more than 5,000 hungry souls.

Many people believe Jesus used his divine powers to multiply the loaves. Others believe he was able to entice the multitudes to open their belongings and share the food they brought for themselves. Maybe it's one or the other or a little bit of both. However the miracle may have unfolded that day, it's important to hold on to the command Jesus gives to his disciples when they first show concern for the hungry crowd. Jesus tells them to give them something to eat and asks them how many loaves they have. The miracle takes place only after the disciples look within themselves and to one another to see what they can offer.

Imagine for a moment what went on in the minds and hearts of the people. They saw the disciples give Jesus the food they had rather than keeping it for themselves. Perhaps they were moved to share what they brought as well. "How many loaves have you? Go and see," said Jesus to the disciples (Mark 6:38a, NRSV). It is time now for the people to take this question to heart, turn toward one another, and see what they have to bring to the table.

Jesus has arranged the people in groups for good reason. They are in a position to see one another face-to-face. They can see who has food and who needs it. They can make sure that no one in the group goes hungry. If they see someone offering their food with others, they may be moved to do the same. They can work cooperatively for the good of the group to assure that all are fed. And this is exactly what happens. More than 5,000 people eat their fill, and the leftover food fills 12 baskets.

This Gospel story has a great deal to offer those of us walking the way of Christian discipleship today. Let's begin with the crowd standing before Jesus. Like them, our bellies rumble with hunger. We hunger for an end to the rising tide of violence in our world. We hunger for ways to nonviolently transform the chaos and calamity of these troubled times. We are willing to work cooperatively with those around us for the sake of the common good.

We can see ourselves in the disciples as well. We are concerned about the well-being of those in need. We turn to Jesus in prayer, thinking we can't possibly find enough resources among us to address the enormous need at hand. Jesus reminds us that we must look not only to him but to ourselves and to one another to take stock of what each of us has to offer.

We begin by asking ourselves the question Jesus asks his disciples. "How many loaves have you? Go and see." We look not in the bread boxes of our kitchens but in the breadbaskets of our souls. What gifts do we have that we can bring to the table to transform these troubled times? What abilities has God given us to be shared for the good of others? What skills have we developed as we've grown? And how do we use these gifts in our work for peace?

"To each is given the manifestation of the Spirit for the common good," writes St. Paul (1 Cor 12:7, NRSV). When we think of this in terms of the spirituality of nonviolence, it means that each of us is given spiritual gifts that we are to use in our work for peace. Some of us are good at coming up with fresh ideas and creative approaches, so we bring this to the table. Others are good at organizing, writing, or educating, and so we bring that to the table. Still others have the gift of prophecy, visioning, or administration, and so we bring that to the table.

In addition to these types of gifts, we bring the attributes that are part of us as well. Some of us may have an abundance of patience or a wealth of wisdom that we've developed throughout our lives. Others may have the gift of listening deeply and compassionately to another. Still others may have a disarming nature that helps people to feel at ease in their presence. And so on and so on.

Whatever our gifts may be, we can use them to enrich our work for peace. We offer them in the manner of Jesus in this Gospel story. Jesus looked first to heaven before blessing the gifts given to him. So, too, we bring our gifts before our God. We acknowledge the need for God's holy touch upon these humble gifts. We then place our gifts along with others who are bringing their gifts to the table. Our gifts combined with others strengthen the spirituality of nonviolence, and its power grows.

The power that enlivens the spirituality of nonviolence is the power that flows through this Gospel story. It's a power that is unique and vastly different from other types of power. In today's world, power is often treated as a scarce commodity. Those who have power often want to hold on to it tightly. They act as if their power will somehow be less if they choose to share it with others. The power in this miracle has just the opposite effect. The further the food is distributed among the group, the more the power of the miracle grows. A modicum of food feeds a multitude of people. And a moment of absence becomes a moment of abundance as Jesus reveals the power of nonviolence for all to behold.

The power of nonviolence is not a power withheld from others but one that is willingly shared with others. It is generous rather than greedy, a power that longs to spread like a loaf of bread longs to be broken. The more it is shared, the greater it becomes. The further it spreads among a group of people, the more it grows and its ability to transform becomes greater.

We grow as well each time we open ourselves up to the spirit of non-violence stirring within. When the spirit of nonviolence finds its way into the soul of any one of us, it becomes like leaven, wanting to expand. It is the yeast that stretches us, body and soul, so that we become more than we were before we discovered it. This spirit enriches our lives with its presence so that we might enrich the lives of others with its power. In this way, we become more than we were before we discovered nonviolence. And the spirituality of nonviolence becomes more than it was before it discovered us.

This dynamic can be plainly seen in the lives of those who are luminaries in the field of nonviolence. When I think of people like Gandhi, Etty Hillesum, Thomas Merton, Dorothy Day, or Dan and Phil Berrigan, I think of how each of them grew as a person because of nonviolence. They opened themselves up to the spirituality of nonviolence and became more because of it. I think, too, of how each of them enriches our understanding of nonviolence through their writings and their lived expression of it. The spirituality of nonviolence mingled with the fiber of their being and became more through them. The same is true of all those nonviolent luminaries, past and present, who we look to for guidance and inspiration.

And the same is true for each of us, whether we consider ourselves to be luminaries, leaders, or lowly followers. I remember two occasions when I grew because of nonviolence and was able to bring its spirit into conflicts where it was greatly needed. Both of these situations occurred in nonprofit organizations where I worked. I was a leader in both settings, and it so happened that another leader in the organization took an action toward me that I believed to be unjust. These actions were done in a public manner, and others in the organizations quickly formed opinions about what was happening. A good number of people believed I had been treated unjustly, and some of them were incensed. The eyes of many people were upon me, watching to see how I would respond.

Let me be clear that my response certainly wasn't perfect. I had to wade through my own pain and anger as I considered what to do. I faced a nonviolent moment, and the way forward was unclear. Yet my foundation in nonviolence held me firm. As I prayed, God kept nudging me toward a nonviolent response. I knew that I wanted to act for the good of all involved, including those I believed were acting unjustly toward me. So I reached into the breadbasket of my soul to see what was there to offer and found what I needed. I found a way to be a presence for peace in public while addressing the pain of the injustice in private. I was able to take steps toward reconciliation instead of retaliation. And through my actions others were inspired to do the same.

As I've reflected on these experiences, I've realized I couldn't have acted in a spirit of nonviolence if I hadn't first built a spiritual foundation of nonviolence. This inner foundation helped me to act on behalf of the greater good, and it gave me more of the qualities I needed at that time. I found a way to practice patience with all that was happening. I was more able to channel my anger in a positive way and more capable of reaching out to receive the support I needed. I was able to be more understanding with myself and more accepting of the uncertainty that came as a consequence of all that happened.

The more we open ourselves up to the power of nonviolence, the more we become the leaven of nonviolence for others. In the process, we come to know the spirit of "more" that flows through the spirituality of nonviolence.

The "more" of nonviolence is not to be confused with the "more" that is craved in our have-it-all society, a ravenous hunger for more stuff, more wealth, and more power. The "more" of nonviolence is about generating more of the stuff that peace is made of. More love. More understanding. More compassion. More equality. More right relationship. We bear witness to the "more" of nonviolence whenever we strive for more freedom, more justice, more wholeness, and more peace. The more we strive for peace, the more we strengthen the spirituality of nonviolence. And the more we transform our society.

In their pastoral message on violence, the US Catholic bishops called us to the "more" of nonviolence, saying,

> The Catholic community is in a position to respond to violence
> and the threat of violence with new commitment and creativity . . .

> Our society needs both more personal responsibility and
> broader social responsibility to overcome the plague of violence in
> our land and the lack of peace in our hearts.[1]

These words remind us that we have a responsibility as Christians to bring more nonviolence into our homes and our communities. When we practice nonviolence in our daily lives, we bring more right living into our world. We engage our adversaries nonviolently and bring a little more peace to dwell upon our planet. We raise our voices in a common cry against intolerance in an effort to bring more understanding into our communities. The more people engage in nonviolent living, the more nonviolence is recognized as a viable tool of social change. Little by little, the "more" of nonviolence makes its way into the world in which we live. And the arc of the universe bends a little more toward justice.

The sense of "more" that we experience through our work for nonviolence resembles the miracle of the loaves and fishes in another way. In this story, Jesus encounters a situation of absence and he transforms it into a time of abundance. In a similar way, the spirituality of nonviolence brings the gifts of abundance to situations where justice and peace are absent. Where there is an absence of community, nonviolence pours a cup overflowing with communion. Where there is an absence of dialogue and listening, nonviolence offers abundant tools for communication. Where there is a chasm created by conflict, nonviolence brings cooperation, enough to bridge the divide. Again and again, absence is transformed by abundance as we bring our gifts to the table and offer them for the good of our world.

The story of the loaves and fishes has long been regarded as a miracle with eucharistic overtones. The act of Jesus blessing the bread then breaking and sharing it resembles the eucharistic meal Christians share today. The power that is present as the food becomes more than enough to feed everyone brings a transcendent quality to the story. Everyone there experienced the amazing grace that flowed through the crowd as the food multiplied. They tasted the bread of transformation. They glimpsed a vision of a world where all have enough to eat. And they experienced the joy that comes when absence is transformed into abundance to create a table of plenty.

Like the transcendent spirit in this miracle, so, too, there is a transcendent quality that arises when the power of nonviolence is shared. When we join with others in nonviolent actions, we experience a dynamic that

---

1. US Conference of Catholic Bishops, *Confronting a Culture of Violence,* Section V, "We Can Be More Than We Are," and Section VI, "Conclusion."

carries us beyond ourselves. The power that rises up from a group of people engaged in a transformation-seeking action lifts our souls to higher ground. We breathe in the air that flows through God's realm of peace. We taste the new creation that we seek. We transcend the state of the world as it is and arrive for a moment at the threshold of the world we desire.

The bonds we develop by working for peace with others have an air of transcendence as well. We move from glimpsing the beloved community to becoming beloved community. We form bonds of discipleship that are deepened by the costs of discipleship we encounter upon the journey. In the company of each other, we stoke the fires that fuel our work for peace. The flame in my heart is fueled by the flame that burns in your heart, and yours is kindled by the flame of someone else. These flames strengthen the bonds that bind us to one another. And in the union of our burning hearts, the glow of God's glory brightens.

In 1985, I visited El Salvador at a time when the country was being torn apart by civil war. One night, I attended an all-night prayer vigil at the Catholic cathedral in San Salvador. The vigil brought together religious leaders and followers from throughout the city who were working nonviolently for an end to the war. Hour after hour, I listened to amazing stories of courage. A mother crossing a dangerous battlefield to deliver food to a family member on the other side. Women demanding that the government tell them where their disappeared sons had been taken. Women and men, religious and lay, together risking their lives on behalf of the peaceful society they believed in even as combat exploded all around.

I remember thinking how dangerous it was simply for these people to gather. Most were hated by government leaders and accused of sympathizing with the rebels. How easy it would have been for members of the military to storm the church and extinguish them in one fell swoop, a prospect that was to me more than a little unnerving. But they remained undaunted. "By coming together, we strengthen each other and prove to them that they have no power over us," they explained. Together, they broke the bread of faith and shared the cup of fortitude. By struggling together for peace and striving together in hope, they strengthened the bonds of communion among them.

Our prayer vigil ended at dawn the next morning with the sharing of Eucharist. The blessing and breaking of bread that morning was enriched by all the sacred moments shared throughout the night. This group of nonviolent disciples had stoked the flame of community burning in their hearts.

They had looked within the breadbaskets of their souls to name what they had to bring to the table. They had looked into the faces of one another to discover what they could give collectively to their nonviolent struggle. In this way they multiplied the power of nonviolence within and among them. This was the body of Christ, renewed and ready to go forth as the bread of nonviolence, to be broken and shared with a nation hungering for peace.

The power I experienced in the midst of this community is the same power I've experienced with small communities engaged in nonviolent transformation in many places. Each community looks different. Yet the power that is palpable in the midst of them is very much the same. It's the power I tasted with small Christian communities in Chile engaged in the struggle for liberation. It's the power I've experienced with communities of peacemakers across the US working to overcome social injustice. It's the power that flowed through the groups of people that participated in the miracle of the loaves and fishes. It's the power of nonviolence that grows in the context of community.

During my years as the national coordinator of Pax Christi USA, I had many opportunities to be with local and regional Pax Christi communities. These communities consist of peacemakers who meet regularly using the Pax Christi model of prayer, study, and action. They are grounded in God through prayer and rooted in the spirituality of nonviolence. They are informed on issues of injustice and the practice of nonviolence through their study. And they are engaged in creative actions in their communities that flow from prayer, study, and a resilient spirit.

It didn't take long for me to recognize that these local groups form the heart and soul of the national Catholic movement for peace. They are the leaven of nonviolence rising up in their communities. They reveal clearly why peacemaking is not meant to be a private affair. Each of us individually can impact our world in positive ways. But the power of what we can do together is so much more than what we can do alone. And the sustenance we need to enliven our peacemaking is nurtured and strengthened in the context of community.

In the midst of groups such as these, I came to understand more fully what Jesus meant when he said to the disciples, "How many loaves have you? Go and see." When we gather as communities of nonviolent disciples, we aren't looking beyond ourselves to find the power we seek. We are looking within ourselves. We are looking within one another. We are figuring out what each of us brings to the table. We are stoking the flames of our faith. We are discovering the "more" of nonviolence. And we discover that the power of nonviolence is more than enough to transform our world.

Dan Berrigan, SJ, one of the bright lights of the peace movement, knows well the strength of this power and its promise for our world. Speaking of the power generated by communities of nonviolence, he said, "[T]here has to be that overflow that says, 'We are on the move. We have enough to give and we're going to give it. We have more than enough and we can give it.' . . . You can really trust the movement that is producing that kind of overflow of the vessel—it's getting tipped and there's enough for everybody. . . . And if the community is growing and deepening, it will be there. I'm convinced, it will be there."[2]

Let there be no doubt—the community of nonviolence is growing and deepening. It grows each time we contribute to the collective power of nonviolence flowing among us. It deepens as we discover the gifts we've been given to share and bring them to the table. We recognize that we have enough to give and we decide we're going to give it. We realize we have more than enough to give and we *can* give it. We become God's blessing cup, outpoured and overflowing. We become God's breadbasket, growing in fullness the further it is passed. And we multiply the nonviolent power that Jesus stirred in his disciples when he asked, "How many loaves have you? Go and see."

Questions for Reflection and Conversation

1. Do you associate nonviolence with absence or with abundance? Why?

2. What gifts has God given you to be shared with others for the good of our world? How can these gifts be used in working for peace?

3. Do you belong to a community that is committed to nonviolence in some way or have you in the past? If so, what role did/does this community play in your life?

4. Have you experienced the "overflow of power" that can be generated by nonviolent communities? How would you describe this power and what makes it grow?

5. In what ways is nonviolence a leaven in your life and in the life of our world?

2. Svetlik, "Passing the Peace," 37.

3

Midwives of Life and Liberation

I call heaven and earth to witness against you today that I have set before you life and death, blessings and curses. Choose life so that you and your descendants may live . . . (DEUTERONOMY 30:19, NRSV)

THIS TIMELESS COMMAND SPOKEN by Moses is a clarion call to every generation faced with choices between life and death, and that includes all of us hearing these words today. Some of these choices arise in our individual lives as we grapple with decisions about things that are life-giving and those that are deadening or drain life out of us. Others are much more stark in the life-or-death consequences that come with them, especially choices that impact others. Each of them, whether great or small, bears witness to the awesome responsibility God entrusts to us. We are called to be a people who choose life again and again, even when that choice is difficult to make.

The book of Exodus contains a humble story of five faithful women who choose life in a powerful way amidst a climate of death. These women are mentioned only briefly in the book of Exodus. Yet without them Moses may not have become the great liberator he was. Each of them faces a non-violent moment, and they seize these moments in ways that reveal essential aspects of the spirituality of nonviolence. Their actions together remind us that a choice for life made by any one of us today can be a catalyst for others to choose life tomorrow. And sometimes the momentum built through these choices can be enough to change the course of history.

Shortly after the book of Exodus begins, a new king comes to power in Egypt. The Israelites had been living peaceably there up until that time. But with the arrival of this new leader, things suddenly change. "The Israelite people are more numerous and more powerful than we," says Pharaoh (Exod 1:9, NRSV). Fearing their growing numbers and power, Pharaoh subjects the Israelites to lives of servitude by forcing them to labor long and hard. Despite Pharaoh's oppression of the Hebrew people, their numbers continue to grow. Fear of the Israelites spreads throughout the land "so that the Egyptians came to dread the Israelites" (Exod 1:12, NRSV).

Pharaoh decides he must do something decisive to stop the Israelites from increasing in number, so he devises a sinister plan. He calls before him two Hebrew midwives named Shiprah and Puah and orders them to kill in his name. "When you act as midwives to the Hebrew women, and see them on the birthstool," commands Pharaoh, "if it is a boy, kill him; but if it is a girl, she shall live" (Exod 1:16, NRSV).

Imagine being faced with such an agonizing dilemma. Pharaoh has ordered these midwives accustomed to cradling newborns to kill them instead. If this isn't bad enough, they are ordered to kill *Hebrew* children, their own flesh and blood. How can these givers of life suddenly become takers of life? They are faced with a profound choice between life and death. To obey Pharaoh would be to go against the very essence of who they are. Yet to defy Pharaoh could lead to severe personal consequences from a king cruel enough to order the killing of infants.

Scripture tells us that the midwives "feared God," biblical language for acting in faithfulness to the God of their knowing. The women know they must act according to what they believe deep within their being, so they seize the nonviolent moment. In what Scripture scholar Walter Wink calls the first recorded act of civil disobedience, Shiprah and Puah "did not do as the king of Egypt commanded them, but they let the boys live" (Exod 1:17, NRSV).[1]

What courage these women display in taking this action! As Hebrews, they are well acquainted with the oppression being inflicted upon their people. Yet they find within themselves the amazing audacity to stand up to Pharaoh, their oppressor. By standing up to him they stand up to the empire that he leads. And through their actions they create a defining moment. These deliverers of life now deliver nonviolent resistance into the pages of Scripture for the first time.

1. Wink, *Engaging the Powers*, 244.

Pharaoh learns of the defiance of these women and summons them to account for their actions. "Why have you done this," he demands to know, "and allowed the boys to live?" (Exod 1:18, NRSV). These wily women come up with an explanation that will be difficult for Pharaoh to refute. "Because the Hebrew women are not like the Egyptian women," they cunningly reply, "for they are vigorous and give birth before the midwife comes to them" (Exod 1:19, NRSV). Their answer is brilliant. Pharaoh knows nothing of how Hebrew women give birth. So how can he possibly know if the women's answer is fact or fiction?

Shiprah and Puah have outsmarted Pharaoh and he realizes that he cannot accomplish his death wish through these two faith-filled women. God recognizes Shiprah and Puah for choosing life and sets them among God's chosen. "God dealt well with the midwives; and the people multiplied and became very strong" (Exod 1:20, NRSV).

Shiprah and Puah reveal a face of nonviolence that resists cooperating with evil and refuses to be co-opted by it. Two women, small in number yet majestic in spirit, show us that the way of nonviolence is firm in its resolve to withstand the advances of evil. They were less concerned about the cost to themselves if they resisted and more concerned about the cost to others if they didn't. By their bravery, Shiprah and Puah become catalysts who create an opening for life where there was none. Their actions open the door for others to follow their example, and not a moment too soon. For Pharaoh was hardly finished.

Intent upon his death mission, Pharaoh issues a new order, saying, "Every boy that is born to the Hebrews you shall throw into the Nile, but you shall let every girl live" (Exod 1:22, NRSV). Sometime after this Moses is born, a Hebrew boy who by decree should be tossed into the river Nile. Yet his mother, Jochebed, desperately wants to spare the life of her child. Surely she's heard about the nonviolent resistance of the Hebrew midwives. It's possible they were present at the birth of Moses.[2] So Jochebed decides to seize the nonviolent moment by bravely resisting Pharaoh's order. She refuses to toss Moses into the river and quietly hides him instead.

Jochebed reveals a face of nonviolence that shows great care and even caution. There are times when nonviolence must do its work quietly. Time spent in a secluded place creates room to breathe, shore up resources, or ponder a next step. Sometimes the way of nonviolence seeks a secluded place like a fertile egg seeks a womb, in need of a space to grow an idea, give

2. Winter, *WomanWitness*, 16.

shape to a design, wait for the stirrings of wisdom, or ready itself for the time when it will emerge once again into the fray.

Jochebed conceals her son for three months, until "she could hide him no longer" (Exod 2:3, NRSV). Perhaps it was getting too hard to keep his birth a secret. Perhaps he had been discovered and she knew it was only a matter of time before Pharaoh sent someone to dispose of her son. Or perhaps she could hide Moses no longer because she was ready to take another step in the way of nonviolence. The time had come to move her nonviolent resistance out of the shadows and into the light.

When I think of Jochebed during the months she spent hiding Moses, I imagine her creating a plan for the day when she would no longer be able to keep him hidden. We know nothing from Scripture as to what went on within her mind and heart. But she, like every Hebrew mother at that time, must have longed wholeheartedly for her son to live. She had time enough to think about what she might do. I imagine her coming up with the details of a plan as she quietly considered how it would proceed and when to set the plan in motion.

When the time seems right, Jochebed fashions a sturdy basket, puts Moses into it, and places the basket in the reeds along the bank of the river to protect him from the current. She who spent three months hoping her son would not be discovered now hopes with every ounce of her being that he will be.

Jochebed seizes her second nonviolent moment in a way that teaches us pragmatic lessons about the spirituality of nonviolence. When we have a particular goal in mind, the way of nonviolence calls us to ponder our steps carefully. We know that good planning has a much better chance of success than good intentions do. So we seriously consider the who, what, when, where, why, and how of our actions, planning with care and deliberation to intensify the impact of our work.

As Jochebed places Moses in the river, the sister of Moses (known to be Miriam) stands "at a distance, to see what would happen to him" (Exod 2:4, NRSV). But Miriam will not remain at a distance for long. The time has come for her to emerge from the shadows into the light as well.

Sometime thereafter, Pharaoh's daughter comes to the river, notices the basket and finds the infant boy within. "This must be one of the Hebrews' children," she says as she takes in what she has discovered (Exod 2:6c, NRSV). Imagine what goes through her mind and heart at this moment. She must realize that the child lying before her is not a newborn.

And when she does she realizes a whole lot more. This means that someone refused to throw this baby boy into the Nile when he was born. Someone has hidden the child ever since. And that means someone had the courage to resist her father's orders.

As Pharaoh's daughter ponders all of this, Miriam enters into the story. She brings to this nonviolent moment her raw desire that her brother might live and every drop of courage that courses through her veins. With the full-fledged freedom of a child, Miriam throws caution to the wind as she asks, "Shall I go and get you a nurse from the Hebrew women to nurse the child for you?" (Exod 2:7, NRSV).

Miriam's question is the spark that sets this story aflame with the possibility of transformation. What Miriam is really asking is, "Will you join with me and my mother and the Hebrew midwives in nonviolently resisting the slaughter of innocents? Will you stand up to your father's death-dealing edict in defense of life? Won't you use your royal power to spare the life of my brother?"

Miriam is asking the unthinkable. By doing so, she reminds us that the spirituality of nonviolence knows no bounds. It brings tomorrow's possibilities to today's reality by daring to imagine the unimaginable. It expands every narrow-minded "no way" with the breadth of "what if." It forges ahead fearlessly and with great determination. The way of nonviolence stretches far and wide enough to touch even those we may believe are beyond its reach.

Miriam shows us that we must never underestimate the power of suggestion in the midst of a nonviolent moment. A person standing in the uncertainty of such a moment faces a difficult choice and is vulnerable. The power of suggestion can be a very influential tool. Having someone plead for mercy may be exactly what the person needs to make the difficult choice for nonviolence.

Pharaoh's daughter didn't expect a dilemma that would rock her world of royalty when she came to the river. Now that she has seen this child, does she wash her hands of the situation and return to life as usual? Or does she risk turning her world upside down in order to have mercy? Sparing the life of this boy would mean defying her father and accepting the consequences, whatever they may be. And they could be harsh, coming from a man who has ordered the slaughter of innocents not once but twice.

As Pharaoh's daughter beholds this fragile child, something is moved deep within her. Perhaps she has heard about the Hebrew midwives who dared to resist her father's death order. This baby before her is living proof that someone else has refused to comply with her father's command. Who knows how many other Hebrews in the land were hiding their newborns! And this precocious girl standing before her has mustered the audacity to suggest that she, too, disobey her father's decree.

In a profound act of defiance, Pharaoh's daughter casts aside her father's order and casts her lot with the women whose actions have brought her to this moment. With the life of Moses hanging on her answer, she replies to Miriam simply, saying, "Yes" (Exod 2:8, NRSV).

"Yes," meaning, "Yes, go get someone to nurse him. . . . Yes, I will join with you and the other women in resisting the evil order of my father. . . . Yes, I will choose life for this child and create an opening for life to prevail in a culture of death." The "yes" of Pharaoh's daughter is the climax in the story of these five women who have courageously chosen life. Each of them has seized the nonviolent moment in her own way. And together they have disrupted the deadly plans of empire long enough to spare the life of Moses.

The choice of Pharaoh's daughter is extraordinary. This woman leads a life of privilege. She doesn't have to show concern for someone of another class and nation. She doesn't need to get involved. She certainly doesn't need to go against her father's order! Yet she does. She makes a selfless choice on behalf of a people not her own. And she demonstrates what can happen when the spirit of nonviolence breaks into our lives with its groundbreaking power.

We break new ground whenever we open ourselves up to the groundbreaking power of nonviolence. Sometimes this power will be strong and surprising, as it was for Pharaoh's daughter. At other times it may be more subtle and gentle. However the spirituality of nonviolence breaks up our fallow ground, it is an invitation to grow. We may take one small step along the way of nonviolence. Or we may forge ahead fearlessly into the unknown, holding fast to our faith. However we respond to the nonviolent stirrings within, the ground of our being cracks open as new growth sprouts forth. We give ourselves to the way of nonviolence and let it lead us where it may. And it just may lead us in directions we never imagined we would go.

Miriam wastes no time in finding someone to nurse her brother as she runs straight to her mother. Pharaoh's daughter says to Jochebed, "Take this child and nurse it for me, and I will give you your wages"(Exod 2:9, NRSV). Moses returns to the breast of his mother, and Jochebed is paid to be his wet nurse.

The prayers of Jochebed have been answered. Moses is rescued from the reeds and returned to her loving embrace. Her nonviolent actions along with Miriam's have secured a future for her son. And nonviolence has secured a place in history as a force strong enough to bring the grace of transformation to the gates of empire.

There's a delightful dose of irony running through this Scripture story. Both of Pharaoh's deadly decrees command the killing of infant boys. Both allow newborn girls to live. Yet it is the actions of five females that spare the life of Moses. It is Moses who is sent by God to liberate the Israelites from their oppression. And through Moses the Israelites are freed from the bondage first imposed upon them by Pharaoh.

This story contains great wisdom about how we are to choose life before the powers of death. Pharaoh can be viewed as a symbol of leaders from powerful nations and empires today. These leaders may not directly order the killing of infants. But how often do they make decisions that result in the death of innocents, either directly or indirectly? Pharaoh felt threatened by the growing number of Israelites in his land. Today's pharaohs feel threatened by the growing number of forces deemed to be a menace to their lands or power. And so they implement death-dealing tactics and policies in an effort to neutralize these threats.

When the powers that be are in the business of death, the God of life calls us to take action. We answer this call with the courage of the five Exodus women. And we learn from the wisdom contained in the way each woman seizes her nonviolent moment.

The example of Shiprah and Puah reveals the pioneering spirit of nonviolence and teaches us an important lesson. When there is no path, the way of nonviolence blazes a trail for others to follow. There are times when nonviolence calls us to veer off the beaten path and create the way by walking it. The terrain may be rough and rocky. We may not know where we are going. But like these women we know deep within that we must act, and we rely on our moral compass to be our guide.

Shiprah and Puah seize their nonviolent moment with the fortitude of faith. They align themselves not with Pharaoh but with a God who cherishes life. They demonstrate a faith that professes a deep commitment to God's law of love. This is the faith that forms the firm foundation of the spirituality of nonviolence. It flows from the heart of a God who has acted tenderly, tenaciously, and tirelessly in defending life throughout the course of salvation history. And it flows from the heart of a faith whose leaders have written, "Respect for life is . . . a fundamental moral principle flowing from our teaching on the dignity of the human person."[3]

There are times when nonviolence calls us to follow in the footsteps of Jochebed, whose actions were quite different from those of the midwives. By keeping Moses out of sight for three months, I believe this courageous woman gave herself time and space to come up with a plan that had a very specific purpose in mind. Her witness reminds us that there are times when we must approach our actions with a spirit that is deliberating and discerning. We take the time and the space we need to plan. We think about and prayerfully consider the purpose of our actions and the outcome we are seeking.

When we take time to discern the goal of our actions, we engage in our work for peace with a greater sense of purpose. And we communicate this sense of purpose in the way our action is carried out. Over the years I've been involved in many nonviolent actions and campaigns. Those that have a clear purpose reflect this in the way the action or campaign is carried out. The tone of the action is focused. The intention is communicated clearly. There is a sense that all involved are united around a common goal. If the action continues over a period of time, the leaders pay attention to each step of their planning. They consider what has been accomplished, what has failed, and what is needed to continue moving toward the goal.

I've also been a part of nonviolent actions where there is no clear or unifying sense of purpose. These actions often come across as unfocused. A sense of purpose is not communicated in the way the action is carried out. If the action continues over a period of time, there's often no clear sense of how one step relates to the next. The message becomes muddled, and the impact of the action is diminished.

When we are up against powers that plan their actions with great cunning, our chances of success are greater if we go about our work in ways that are focused and conducted with a sense of purpose. When I look at nonviolent campaigns that have been the most successful over the years, a clear pattern emerges. Those that accomplished their goals went about their work in a way that was sustained and strategic.

This type of nonviolence was implemented in very effective ways during the civil rights movement. Week after week, nonviolent protesters went to lunch counters to sit where they were not allowed by law to sit. When

---

3. US Conference of Catholic Bishops, *Confronting a Culture of Violence*, Section I, "Introduction."

one band of protesters was arrested, another wave immediately moved in. There was no letup. Month after month this continued until the protesters achieved their goal and the lunch counters became integrated. I remember this kind of sustained nonviolence being used in New York City years ago after the killing of an unarmed black man by police officers. Day after day there were civil disobedience actions at city hall calling for justice. The persistence of protestors eventually forced the city to bring charges against the officers and put them on trial for their actions.

Coordinated campaigns and sustained actions can be a lot of work. Yet these types of actions have shown that they can accomplish great things. They build momentum and p1ower. They disrupt business as usual. They make nonviolence a pervasive force tenaciously seeking to achieve its purpose. They send a message that we intend to be a relentless presence for peace that will not be easily turned away. In its finest hour, sustained and strategic nonviolence can generate power strong enough and momentum sweeping enough to halt the advance of empire and hasten the advent of peace.

This happened when President Obama called for military intervention against Syria in response to the 2013 gas attacks that led to massive death and suffering of the Syrian people. As soon as peacemakers received word of his intentions, they began to mobilize. The message was focused and consistent—military intervention will only escalate the violence and will not solve the problems there. The call was clear—diplomatic action through sanctions and concerted efforts to bring about a cease-fire. Social media spread the word far and wide to Americans to contact their members of Congress. And people responded.

Within just a few days there was a clear majority of voices crying out against military intervention and calling for peace. These voices received a major thrust when Pope Francis called for an international day of prayer and fasting, and people of faith throughout the world responded. In less than a week, a diplomatic resolution was being considered and threats of intervention had stopped. The hand of empire had been stayed by a huge outpouring of empathy.

This campaign was short in duration, yet it was strategic in the way that the message was so clearly focused. It was coordinated through concerted actions directed toward Congress. And it was sustained by the intensity of people crying out for peace in public and praying in private day after day.

In addition to being strategic, our nonviolent actions must be alive with the kind of creativity that led Miriam to make an outrageous request of Pharaoh's daughter. When we transcend "inside-the-box" thinking we quickly discover the freedom that frolics outside the box. These types of actions embrace a spirit willing to leap into the great beyond with boldness and daring. And when we bring to our actions the spirit of the unimaginable, unimaginable things can happen.

Dorothy Day and Peter Maurin brought the spirit of the unimaginable to their work, and the Catholic Worker Movement was born. A French laywoman and a French bishop brought the unimaginable spirit of reconciliation in the wake of World War II, and Pax Christi, the international Catholic peace movement, was born. Rosa Parks, the Rev. Martin Luther King Jr., and others brought the unimaginable spirit of equality to the segregated South, and the civil rights movement was born. We must ask ourselves— where is the spirit of the unimaginable stirring in the work of peacemaking today? How is it stirring in our hearts? What is the movement that is begging to be born at this nonviolent moment?

When the spirit of the unimaginable is present, the unlikeliest people can become partners in transformation. Miriam reached out to the daughter of Pharaoh, a very unlikely ally, and invited her to be an active participant in transformation. We must remember that the goal of our work for peace is not victory over the pharaohs and emperors of our day (or their relatives). The goal is a transformation that will only be complete when both oppressed and oppressor are free.

Last but hardly least, we bring to our nonviolent action the courageous and compassionate spirit of Pharaoh's daughter. This noble woman doesn't brush Miriam off as we might expect from someone in her position. She reaches beyond any selfish concerns and creates a space in her heart to grant Miriam's merciful request. She breaks her ties with the evil ways of empire, at least for a moment. When she does, she experiences a breakthrough. She breaks through the oppression that is holding this child hostage. And she discovers a way to relinquish the death sentence imposed upon Moses.

Of the women in this story, perhaps it is Pharaoh's daughter who speaks most profoundly to those of us living in the world's most powerful nation today. Shiprah, Puah, Jochebed, and Miriam were all Hebrew women, and so they were among those oppressed by Pharaoh. But Pharaoh's daughter was one who held a powerful and privileged place in society. She had to choose between being faithful to the command given by her father or being faithful to her conscience. She was forced to choose between solidarity with her country or solidarity with those being oppressed by her country. This kind of dilemma is not uncommon to those of us who find ourselves living in the United States today.

I remember a lesson I learned during the time I spent as a volunteer in Belize after college. I lived and worked among people who did not have the privileges I took for granted. A number of us who were volunteering began to question what we wanted to do with our lives after our time of service. Our hearts had broken open in new ways, creating space for seeds of something more to grow. We talked with our Belizean mentors, and their advice to us was clear. "Take what you have experienced here back home with you," they said. "Use it to change the policies of your government that are contributing in a big way to the oppression you see here."

This is the work of those of us who live with the blessing and burden of privilege. We are called to be faithful to our God who loves the poor as well as the privileged. We have the power to cry out on behalf of those whose voices are silenced. "An ethic of respect for life," wrote the bishops in their pastoral letter, "should be a central measure of all our institutions— community, economic, political and legal."[4] We are called to advocate for those whose lives are compromised by the conduct of our nation. We must follow the voice of our conscience by refusing to support actions that lead to suffering and oppression. Our dual identity as inhabitants of this wealthy nation and nonviolent Christian disciples compel us to work for the transformation of institutions and individuals alike.

When Pharaoh's daughter said "yes" to nonviolence by saying "yes" to Miriam, she issued a command that resounds throughout the ages. Her "yes" commissions faithful followers to rise up in defense of life wherever it is threatened by the powers that be. This command echoes from one generation to the next, encouraging us to persist in our efforts. It is the "yes" that reminds us the actions we take can stir someone else to action. It is the "yes" that resounds in the heart of a God who longs for fullness of life for all.

Each time we respond to this summons, we choose life by opening the door to a future that looks very different from life as we know it. We choose a life where control by the privileged gives way to collaboration by the many. We choose a life where security is fostered not by stockpiling

4. Ibid., Section II, "A Culture of Violence."

weapons but by safeguarding the common good. We choose a life where wealth is measured not by the riches of individuals but by the resources of the community. We become midwives bringing to birth a world where the coveting of power gradually yields itself to a covenant of peace.

Let us remember that five women, small in number but stalwart in spirit, became midwives of liberation long ago. And through our laboring for peace we can become midwives of liberation once again.

Questions for Reflection and Conversation

1. What, in particular, struck you about the nonviolent resistance of the Exodus women? What lessons do their examples hold for you?

2. Have you ever refused to cooperate with something that violated your faith or conscience or witnessed others engaging in this type of resistance? What are your thoughts/feelings about this type of nonviolent witness?

3. Have you ever engaged in nonviolent resistance in a private way? Have you taken steps to make your resistance more public? Why/why not?

4. Where is the spirit of the unimaginable stirring in the work of peacemaking today? How is it stirring in your heart?

5. Do you think the times in which we live call us to be more sustained and strategic in our work for nonviolence? Why/why not? If so, how might we accomplish this?

6. Have you ever been stirred to take action because of the nonviolent witness of another person? Have you taken a nonviolent action that encouraged someone else to act in a spirit of nonviolence as well?

4

Practicing Forgiveness in an Unforgiving World

All of this from God, who ransomed us through Christ—and made us ministers of that reconciliation. This means that through Christ, the world was fully reconciled again to God, who didn't hold our transgressions against us, but instead entrusted us with this message of reconciliation. (2 CORINTHIANS 5:18–19, TIB)

WHEN I FIRST READ this Scripture passage, it captured me. How amazing to think God entrusts us with something as important as the ministry of reconciliation. This ministry holds the possibility of healing and redemption for a world sickened by hatred and division. At the same time, this God-given responsibility is daunting. We are called to live out an awesome, countercultural mission in a world increasingly inclined toward retribution.

Being messengers and ministers of reconciliation means we need to be well-practiced in the work of forgiveness. Forgiveness breathes new life into strained relationships and discovers in brokenness the pieces of wholeness. It loosens hearts constricted by anger and leads the way toward healing. When wrongdoing strews its wreckage across the roadway of life, forgiveness clears the path to create a way forward.

Forgiveness held a sacred place in the life and ministry of Jesus. He granted forgiveness freely and frequently. Jesus tells Peter to forgive a wrongdoer not seven times but seventy times seven (Matt 18:21–22). Those who approach the altar with their gifts are told to go and be reconciled to those they have wronged before making their offering (see Matt 5:23–24). Jesus sups with sinners and extends to them the hand of forgiveness over and over. He teaches the disciples to pray that God forgive them their sins as they forgive those who sin against them (see Luke 11:4). And he announces that he has come "to call not the righteous but sinners" (Matt 9:13b, NRSV).

Jesus revealed the power of forgiveness in many ways throughout his life. Yet it is his death and resurrection that reveal its promise for a world transformed.

Luke's gospel tell us that as Jesus hangs dying upon the cross, he prays to God, saying, "Abba, forgive them. They don't know what they are doing" (Luke 23:34, TIB). These astounding words are spoken as his life and mission are coming to an unjust end. Yet Jesus doesn't do what many of us might do. He doesn't pray for vengeance. He doesn't pray for condemnation. Instead, Jesus transforms a very violent moment into a nonviolent moment. He uses his dying breath to mouth a public message of pardon and sets the stage for a revolutionary faith to take hold.

These words of Jesus appear only in Luke's gospel. Scripture scholars tell us that they do not appear in other ancient authorities, and so it is believed they were a later addition to Scripture. Luke certainly had his reasons for recording them in his Gospel. In doing so, I imagine he had a burning desire for the message of reconciliation to take hold in the heart of the early Christian community. And there is a great need for the Christian community today to embrace this message as well.

After rising from the dead, Jesus immediately reinforces his message of forgiveness. The disciples are gathered together in a locked room, not knowing what to make of the news that Jesus has risen. In the midst of their confusion, Jesus appears to them, saying, "Peace be with you" (John 20:19, NRSV). He then tries to convince this bewildered group that he has truly risen by showing them his hands and his side. Jesus then says a second time, "Peace be with you" (John 20:21, NRSV).

How earth shattering this must have been for the disciples! Not only had Jesus risen from the dead, but his response to all that happened was forgiveness. No chastising the disciples for abandoning him in his moment of need. Instead, he reaches out to them with the peace of God's pardon. Jesus then goes even further. He draws the disciples close and breathes upon them, saying, "Receive the Holy Spirit. If you forgive the sins of any, they are forgiven them; if you retain the sins of any, they are retained" (John 20:22–23, NRSV).

These words form a covenant between Jesus and his disciples. Forgiveness becomes the thread that weaves together his dying and rising and takes a central place in the legacy he leaves for his disciples. Not only does Jesus forgive his followers for denying him and abandoning him. He goes so far as to entrust his forgiven ones with the ministry of reconciliation.

He entrusts this ministry to all of us who follow him today as well. I imagine the disciples hardly felt up to what Jesus was asking of them when they were commissioned. They had failed Jesus and were trying to make sense of all that was happening. They surely weren't ready to be ambassadors of forgiveness! If we find ourselves feeling unready or unable to accept this call today, we know we are in good company. God often calls us in places where we feel most vulnerable and asks us to do things that seem impossible. If we are able to answer the call, God is more than ready to show us the way.

The dying words of Jesus as recorded in Luke's gospel offer insights into the way of forgiveness, especially in difficult times. It's important to pay attention to what Jesus says and what he doesn't say here. Jesus makes it clear that he desires forgiveness. Yet he doesn't take matters into his own hands. He doesn't say to those who are killing him, "I forgive you, for you do not know what you are doing." Rather, Jesus says, "Abba, forgive them. They don't know what they are doing" (Luke 23:34, TIB). He beseeches God to do the forgiving.

Why is it that Jesus asks God to forgive rather than offering forgiveness himself? Perhaps in that tormented time it was too hard for Jesus to forgive on his own. Maybe the anguish was too great or he was simply too weak. Or maybe he was teaching us a lasting lesson about forgiveness. He shows us that the way of forgiveness begins by turning to God in prayer.

The story of Immaculée Ilibagiza demonstrates just how powerful prayer can be in moving our hearts to forgive. Immaculée is a survivor of the 1994 Rwandan genocide. She lost most of her family, including her mother and a beloved brother, in a rampage that killed more than 800,000 people and lasted one hundred days. She survived by hiding in a cramped bathroom in her pastor's house with seven other Tutsi women to escape the slaughter of the Hutus. She pleaded with God in that bathroom for hours on end as prayer became her stronghold. She prayed to survive as death and destruction raged around her. She prayed to drive out the voices of doubt and desperation that threatened her faith in God. And she prayed to somehow forgive those responsible for the genocide.

It took a lot of prayer and spiritual wrestling before she could even think about forgiveness for the killers. Over the long days and nights, Immaculée listened to radio reports of the killings. She heard the cruelty of the killers as they slaughtered innocents beneath her window and searched for more Tutsis in the room outside her door. And she received daily updates from the pastor about the horrors of the Hutu attacks. "I'd never done anything violent to anyone before," Immaculée recalls, "but at that moment I wished I had a gun so that I could kill every Hutu I saw."[1]

Hatred and anger took hold of her heart, and Immaculée filled her days and nights with prayer. She prayed the rosary for hours on end. Over time she grew uncomfortable when she recited the Lord's Prayer. Saying the words "forgive us our trespasses as we forgive those who trespass against us" made her feel like a hypocrite. At first she simply excluded the killers from her mind as she prayed these words of forgiveness. Yet the more she recited these words, the more unsettled her soul became.

One afternoon the killers returned to search the house where Immaculée was hidden. She had been praying the rosary since dawn, asking "for God to give His love and forgiveness to all the sinners of the world. But try as I might I couldn't bring myself to pray for the killers. That was a problem for me because I knew that God expected us to pray for *everyone*, and more than anything, I wanted God on my side."[2]

A voice in her head began to taunt her, saying, *"Why are you calling on God? Don't you have as much hatred in your heart as the killers do? Aren't you as guilty of hatred as they are?"*[3] Immaculée became desperate as the killers came closer to her hiding place. Fearing for her life, she prayed for the killers even though she firmly believed that they deserved to die. She admitted that she didn't know how to forgive them and asked God to teach her.

Immaculée survived her close brush with death, and the answer to her prayers came one night soon after as the killing continued outside her window. She listened in anguish to the cries of an orphaned infant all through the night. The cries gradually grew weaker and eventually stopped, and she knew that the child had died. She prayed for the soul of the child and asked God how she could possibly forgive people cruel enough to kill innocent

1. Ilibagiza, *Left to Tell*, 88.
2. Ibid., 91.
3. Ibid., 92.

children. The answer came loud and clear. *"You are all my children . . . and the baby is with Me now."*[4]

Her closed heart suddenly opened as she recognized the killers were like children. "Their minds had been infected with the evil that had spread across the country, but their *souls* weren't evil. Despite their atrocities, they were children of God, and I could forgive a child, although it would not be easy. . . . "[5] At that moment she prayed that they be forgiven.

After the war ended and she tried to rebuild the pieces of her life, Immaculée visited the imprisoned leader of the gang that killed her mother and brother. The prison guard confronted him with the atrocities he had committed and asked him what he had to say for himself. He broke down sobbing at the sight of Immaculée. Filled with pity, she reached out, touched his hands, offered him her forgiveness, and felt her heart soften. When the flabbergasted guard asked her why she had done this rather than unleash her anger upon him, she said, "Forgiveness is all I have to offer."[6]

Immaculée moved from outright hatred to forgiveness through extensive prayer. She was able to do this by wrestling deep within her soul to forgive the unforgivable. Her story is an inspiration to all of us who practice forgiveness in an unforgiving world. She reminds us that forgiveness is a process that can take a long time and involve a lot of effort. If she can forgive something as heinous as a massacre, surely there is hope for us all.

When I meet with people who are struggling to forgive, I ask them two questions. Are you asking God to show you the way? And are you praying for the person you need to forgive? More often than not, the answer to one or both of these questions is no. I share with them my belief that we must approach forgiveness from a posture of prayer. And I share with them words of wisdom from people much wiser than me.

There is a wonderful piece of advice offered in twelve-step programs that I find helpful when I'm struggling to pray for someone I need to forgive. It is the bold and blunt suggestion to "pray for the bastard." These words may sound jarring at first, especially when we consider using them in the context of prayer. Yet the words are so refreshingly real. We are invited to begin right where we are, standing deep in the muck and mire of our anguish, and from that place to pray. If the best we can do at that moment is to pray for the bastard, then that's what we do. And God will

4. Ibid., 94.

5. Ibid.

6. Ibid., 204.

receive our halting prayer just as eagerly as God receives prayers that are offered wholeheartedly.

There is another piece of twelve-step advice I find helpful when I find myself struggling to forgive. It is the suggestion to "fake it till you make it." When I apply this to my need to forgive, I recognize that I may be incapable of forgiving today. But I can act as if I am forgiving. I can refuse to do or say anything that might cause harm to the person I need to forgive. I can offer prayers for the person and for myself. I can hold fast to my great love for a world united as one, a love that requires that I somehow forgive this person. I can ask that God's merciful love wash over my hardened heart until I am able to forgive.

And I can mouth the prayer of forgiveness that Jesus uttered from the cross. The words "forgive them; they don't know what they are doing" can be a mantra that we repeat over and over when we are trying to forgive. We rest in the assurance that God is offering forgiveness as we allow these words to do their work in us. Over time, our hardened inner spaces slowly begin to soften. The closed places within us gradually begin to open. God understands the anguish wreaking havoc on our hearts. And God desires nothing more than to relinquish us from the grip of our anguish and lead us into the gentle embrace of forgiveness.

So God nudges us to take another step. When I pray for someone that I'm trying to forgive, I imagine myself mouthing the words, "I forgive you" to them. I force myself to push out the words, even when they stick in my throat. When the process of forgiveness is long and arduous, I imagine myself saying "I am forgiving you" rather than "I forgive you." This acknowledges that I am a work in progress. I have begun the process of forgiveness, but I have a long way to go. By repeating these words over time, I gradually grow into them.

Through prayer I come to recognize that the person I'm struggling to forgive is a beloved child of God, just like me. I remember that I am linked to this person as a sister or brother in God's one human family. Each time I entertain an unkind thought or feeling for this person I harm no one but me. The longer I hold on to my pain, the longer I am bound by it. The only way to free my heart from its anguished state is to let go and let God. Let go of the pain and let God tend to my wounds. Let go of the resistance and let God sow seeds of reconciliation within me. Let go of the wrongdoing, and let God show me how to forgive.

The Rev. Martin Luther King Jr. wrote, "Forgiveness is not an occasional act—it is a permanent attitude."[7] Developing a permanent attitude of forgiveness is essential to a ministry of reconciliation. When forgiveness moves from being an act to an attitude, it becomes a part of us. It becomes less of something we do and more of who we are. Slowly but surely, forgiveness becomes a way of life, much like it did for Martin Luther King Jr. He endured hatred and opposition on a regular basis yet somehow found it in his heart to forgive again and again and again. If he hadn't, he couldn't have been the great messenger and minister of reconciliation he was. A permanent attitude of forgiveness made it possible for him to devote himself wholeheartedly to his work.

If we choose to follow the way of nonviolence, then we must strive to cultivate a permanent attitude of forgiveness. We carry in our hearts the intention of forgiveness that Jesus carried in his heart and breathed on his disciples. Forgiveness is something we truly practice and rarely, if ever, perfect. Each time we are wronged by another, we are given another opportunity to practice. The more we practice, the more we grow in our understanding of what a permanent attitude of forgiveness is all about. And our capacity to forgive grows as well.

It's important to remember that a permanent attitude of forgiveness is not the same as a permanent attitude of excusing misdeeds. Forgiveness does not condone transgressions or excuse the sins of the perpetrator. Rather, forgiveness acknowledges wrongdoing and those responsible for it. It acknowledges the pain of those who have been wronged and their longing to seek accountability from their wrongdoers. And, contrary to popular belief, forgiveness does not forget. In the words of Fr. Leonel Narvaez, a Catholic priest who has been involved in Schools of Forgiveness and Reconciliation in some of Colombia's most conflicted areas, "Forgiveness is not forgetting but rather remembering with different eyes."[8]

To remember with different eyes is to gaze upon those responsible for wrongdoing with eyes of mercy rather than malice. It is to hold in our hearts the lessons to be learned from the misdeed rather than holding onto the pain. It is a choice made by beholding wrongdoing in the light of God's love. From this vantage point, we begin to see differently. We recognize that a nonviolent moment arises from the brokenness of a transgression.

7. King, "Love in Action," 38.

8. Fellowship of Reconciliation, "Why is Colombia's the Most Under-reported War in the World?," 5.

We who are troubled by the wrongdoing can choose to hold on tightly to our pain and be tightly held by it in return. Or we can choose the way of forgiveness and thereby release ourselves from the harmful hold of our anguish.

This is what Jesus was trying to convey when he gave the disciples a choice between forgiving or retaining sins. He understood how destructive it can be for us to hold on to sins rather than forgiving them. Jesus understood, too, how hard it can be to forgive, especially when the sins committed are cruel or done in a callous manner. He was profoundly aware of this as he was suffering the pain of his crucifixion, which is why there is another lesson to be learned from the dying words of Jesus. And it is by far the most difficult.

From a place of horror and humiliation Jesus chose forgiveness and stated his belief that his executioners didn't know what they were doing. He uttered this prayer knowing full well that those who opposed him had planned to kill him. He made it clear that no one is beyond the reach of forgiveness. And he made it clear that even the cruelest and most calculating of crimes can be forgiven.

In a post-September 11 world, these words present a clear and uncompromising challenge. Our attitude as a nation certainly hasn't resembled "forgive them, for they know not what they are doing." We have adopted instead an attitude of "destroy them, for they know damn well what they are doing." Our nation has become a superpower willing to attack whenever and wherever it chooses. We are becoming a culture where the language of forgiveness is spoken less as the language of retaliation is heard more. Instead of a permanent attitude of forgiveness, we are cultivating a permanent attitude of aggression.

I was living in the Bronx when the horror of September 11 happened. At that time, the possibility of forgiveness seemed all but impossible. The pain was too raw, the wounds too immense. Even so, we as a people had a choice to make. We could choose to make of the brokenness more brokenness. Or we could choose to move forward in a way that would not impose on others the unspeakable pain imposed on us. We could choose to meld the shattered pieces of our society into a design that aspired toward wholeness. Or we could choose a course of action rooted in retribution and retaliation.

Our national leaders took little time to make their choice as September 11 became the justification for going to war. Thousands died in the attacks of September 11. Many thousands more have died in the US-led attacks that have followed.

A few days after the attacks of September 11, I noticed a poster in the window of a shop in my neighborhood. There in all their grandeur were the gleaming twin towers. Pressed into the belly of these buildings was a photo of the towers reduced to a pile of smoking rubble. Printed boldly beneath the photos were the words, "Stay pissed."

Each time I saw this poster, my heart sank. I knew that "staying pissed" was anathema to the process of healing. Staying pissed is like reopening a wound daily. The wound festers and becomes worse. When we stand with our feet defiantly rooted in our pain, we force our wounds to remain open. Our hearts are not allowed to heal. And our souls become a seedbed for a permanent attitude of aggression to grow.

The prayer of Jesus on the cross cries out today with as much urgency as it did long ago. We are not called to stay pissed. We are called instead to pardon. We turn our gaze toward the outstretched arms of Jesus on the cross and hold fast to his dying prayer, "Forgive them, for they do not know what they are doing." This supplication applies to every sin committed, no matter how heinous. It applies even to crimes as monumental as those that occurred in Rwanda in 1994 and in the United States on September 11, 2001.

No matter how cruel or calculating an action may be, those engaged in it can never know the full extent of the brokenness their actions will cause. They cannot know the depths of pain that embroils the hearts of individuals directly affected by their actions. They cannot fathom every detail of how their actions will impact the future or comprehend how devastating the damage may be. These transgressions are like rocks thrown into a global pond, sending ripples racing outward. God alone can see the distance traveled by these destructive ripples. God alone comprehends the extent of the damage that results. God alone beholds the arc of the universe bending further away from justice each time these transgressions occur.

The only way to right this arc, the only way to bend it back toward justice, is through forgiveness. This is why Jesus reinforces his message of forgiveness immediately after rising from the dead. Jesus knows his disciples are upset and angry over the brutal death he endured and the dismantling of his ministry. He knows they could easily retain this sin deep within their hearts and be held by it in return. But this is not what Jesus needs or wants from them. He needs to unleash the power of forgiveness in the hearts of his disciples so that they can unleash it in the heart of the world. And so Jesus breathes on them the breath of forgiveness as he says, "If you forgive the sins of any, they are forgiven them; if you retain the sins of any, they are retained" (John 20:22–23, NRSV).

Jesus didn't say what the effect of retaining sins would be. Even so, he knew. He knew that holding onto wrongdoing causes the hearts of individuals to become hardened. It causes the heart of society to become callous. It leads to a culture of people holding onto the hatred that poisons their souls. It creates a toxic environment where a spirit of vengeance is nurtured and acts of retaliation are supported. And it inspires a permanent attitude of aggression to grow.

We don't have to look far to see signs of this kind of culture. Our nation has held on tightly to the sins of September 11. And we have been bound by them in return. We have become the most aggressive nation on the face of the planet. Shortly after our national leaders declared an open-ended global war on terror, a US special forces officer stated in no uncertain terms how aggressive we would be. "We will export death and violence to the four corners of the earth in defense of our great nation," he stated with firm resolve.[9]

This statement shows how destructive a permanent attitude of aggression can be. It also shows how utterly essential our work as ministers of reconciliation is for the healing of our nation. A vow to export death and violence across the planet must be met with a vow to promote forgiveness and reconciliation just as far and wide.

There is a story that speaks of a ritual of healing that takes place somewhere in Africa. When a person is bitten by a poisonous snake, a special stone is placed upon the wound. This stone has the power to draw out the venom and the person is healed. The stone is then placed in a milk bath to cleanse it of the venom drawn from the wound. In this way, it is readied for the work of healing the next time it is needed. Not surprisingly, people hold great respect for the power of these stones, and so the stones hold a prominent place in the people's culture.

There are no magic stones we can use to heal a permanent attitude of aggression. And so we must become the healing stones of our society. When we develop within ourselves a permanent attitude of forgiveness, we become stepping stones that guide others in the way of forgiveness. Our ministry of reconciliation can move our nation to let go of the pain of

9. Andreas, *Addicted to War,* 36.

September 11 and begin the process of healing. It can help others to experience the inner freedom that comes through forgiveness.

The repeated action of the stone and its importance in the African culture says something about a permanent attitude of forgiveness. The stone is called upon to draw out the poisonous venom from a wound again and again. A permanent attitude of forgiveness calls us to draw out the poisonous venom of resentment and vengeance from the heart of our society again and again. As difficult as this can be, we are to rise to the occasion each time forgiveness and reconciliation are needed. We begin by working toward forgiveness in our own hearts. And we do our part to help other people make their way slowly and steadily along the path of reconciliation.

After the healing stone does its work, it is placed in a milk bath to ready it for the next healing. Likewise, we must remember that the work of forgiveness and reconciliation is arduous. It becomes especially difficult when we are striving to foster reconciliation in the face of resistance. We must tend to our souls as we strive to foster forgiveness so that we can be renewed and ready ourselves to forgive again.

Our ministry of reconciliation may not be revered like the stone in the African culture. But it is every bit as important. We are a vital part of quelling the venom and vitriol that are poisoning us as a people. We are an essential part of bringing healing to a world increasingly torn apart by retribution. The way of nonviolence chooses the way of absolution rather than the way of absolute reprisal. It reaches beyond the reality of worldwide chaos to forge the possibility of worldwide community.

In his book *No Future Without Forgiveness*, Archbishop Desmond Tutu suggests that reconciliation is essential for the healing of our world. He writes, "Peace is possible, especially if today's adversaries were to imagine themselves becoming friends and begin acting in ways that would promote such a friendship developing in reality."[10] This may sound farfetched, especially on a national or global scale. Years ago, President Bush went so far as to label the leaders of Iraq, Iran, and North Korea as part of an "axis of evil."[11] Imagining sworn enemies as friends sounds utterly impossible.

But who could have imagined Nelson Mandela inviting F. W. de Klerk to serve in the cabinet that led South Africa after apartheid ended in that country? President de Klerk presided over the system of apartheid when Mandela was imprisoned. Yet Mandela invited de Klerk to serve because

10. Tutu, *No Future Without Forgiveness*, 281.

11. Bush, State of the Union Address.

he forgave him for his complicity with the system of apartheid, recognized the common humanity they shared, and envisioned de Klerk as a partner in establishing justice. He chose to forgive the sins done to him rather than retain them. He reached out to befriend his enemy. And he strived to guide his country away from a permanent attitude of aggression.

Can we imagine what our world would be like if it embraced a permanent attitude of forgiveness? World leaders would resolve their differences not by acts of aggression but through gestures of diplomacy. They would come together around a table of reconciliation seeking understanding. Mediation would replace retaliation. Respect would be the foundation of all that would transpire there. A willingness to compromise would be viewed as a sign of strength rather than weakness. We would come to realize that global security lies not in conquest and division but in collaboration and interdependence. The worldwide web of injustice would begin to unravel. And a world torn apart by fury would begin to yield itself to a world coming together through forgiveness.

Jesus knew what he was doing when he commissioned the disciples with the breath of forgiveness. He was bestowing upon them a power greater than any of them could have imagined. He was granting them the power to change the world.

Questions for Reflection and Conversation

1. What does the term "practicing forgiveness" mean to you? How do you practice forgiveness?

2. When you are faced with a choice between forgiving or retaining a sin, which are you more likely to choose? Why?

3. What might it mean to cultivate a permanent attitude of forgiveness in your personal life? In society?

4. Reflect upon/discuss this statement: "Forgiveness is not forgetting but rather remembering with different eyes." Do you agree or disagree? Why?

5. Have you ever struggled to forgive someone for something that is difficult to forgive? What helped you move toward forgiveness?

6. What does it mean to you to be a minister and messenger of reconciliation? What does a ministry of reconciliation offer society?

5

The Wideness of God's Mercy

"THERE'S A WIDENESS IN God's mercy," begins a nineteenth-century hymn, "like the wideness of the sea." This image suggests that there's nothing stingy or narrow about the mercy of God. It's as though there is something in the makeup of God's mercy that longs to broaden its reach. God's mercy is expansive, stretching farther and wider than the eye can see. God's mercy is overflowing, poured out freely and lovingly upon all those in need. No act, no matter how egregious, is beyond the reach of this mercy. And no one, no matter how sinful or shunned by society, can escape God's merciful embrace.

One of my favorite stories about the wideness of God's mercy is John's gospel account of a woman accused of adultery. In this story, God's mercy stretches wide enough to transform a particularly contentious encounter. Along the way, it teaches us important lessons about the role of mercy in the spirituality of nonviolence.

As the story begins, Jesus is teaching a crowd of people when suddenly the scribes and Pharisees barge in. They forcefully bring with them a woman they claim was caught in the act of adultery. Before the eyes of all gathered, they challenge Jesus directly. "Teacher," they implore, "this woman was caught in the very act of committing adultery. Now in the law Moses commanded us to stone such women. Now what do you say?" (John 8:4–5, NRSV).

Without any warning, Jesus is catapulted into a very prickly nonviolent moment. If he advocates to spare this woman's life, he will be contradicting Judaic law, which specifies death as the punishment for a man and a married woman who commit adultery (see Lev 20:10). If he upholds Judaic law and allows the death sentence to proceed, he will be contradicting every merciful teaching he has ever given. The stakes are high for Jesus, and the life of the woman is on the line.

In the midst of this very tense nonviolent moment, what does Jesus do? He seizes it by doing something entirely unexpected. "Jesus bent down," Scripture tells us, "and wrote with his finger on the ground" (John 8:6b, NRSV). What he writes remains a mystery, for Scripture remains silent on the matter. Over the years, Scripture scholars have devised many theories as to what Jesus may have written. These theories often presume that what Jesus wrote played an important role in the outcome of the story. This certainly may be true. But I've always resonated with the wisdom of revered Johannine scholar Rev. Raymond Brown. He made the logical point that if Jesus wrote something important, chances are it would have been recorded in the Gospel account.[1]

If we place our focus on *what* Jesus wrote, we risk missing the significance of the *act* of writing itself. And it is from the act of writing that the nonviolent and transformative power of this story begins to emerge.

At first glance, the action of writing on the ground seems bizarre. We can imagine the scribes and Pharisees wondering, "Why in God's name is he writing on the ground when he's just been asked a life-or-death question?" But as we look more closely at what Jesus is doing, his actions begin to make a great deal of sense. Instead of giving them the hasty verbal reply they want, he responds with an action that speaks much louder than words.

Jesus is sending a message to all gathered that he intends to stand his ground. The scribes and Pharisees have come to the temple uninvited and disrupted his teaching with their agenda. But Jesus refuses to fall into the trap they are setting. He refuses to allow himself to be manipulated by their behavior. Jesus humbly yet clearly conveys that he is unafraid and ready to deal with this challenge on his terms. And the terms he chooses are the terms of nonviolence.

Bending down to write is a marvelous nonviolent tool that Jesus uses to begin to transfigure this confrontation. By doing something entirely unexpected, Jesus uses the element of surprise to diffuse the situation. He shifts the focus of the crowd's attention. Instead of all eyes staring in anticipation at Jesus and the woman, all eyes stare instead at the ground to see

1. Brown, *The Gospel According to John I–XII*, 334.

what he's doing. Wonder and curiosity enter in like a silent sigh of relief, reducing the tension somewhat.

Jesus likely breathes a little easier, too. Now that all eyes are glued to the ground rather than his face, Jesus has some time to think. I imagine him bending down, taking a deep breath, and saying to himself, "How in God's name will I answer this one?" The act of writing in the sand creates the space Jesus needs to assess the situation, take stock of the resources he has, weigh his possible options, and determine his response. It's like taking a step back from the confrontation so as to determine what the next step will be.

There's a lovely symbolism, too, in the way that Jesus approaches this conflict. Bending down to the ground can be viewed as a symbol of Jesus going deep within himself. The act of bending down is similar to a posture of prayer upon bended knee. He humbly bends toward his deepest self and allows his answer to emerge from that place. As he writes in the sand, it's as if Jesus is fervently asking God to write the answer to this dilemma upon the sands of his soul.

Growing impatient, the religious authorities urge Jesus to answer their question. But Jesus needs no urging. He has given himself the space he needs to gain a foothold in this confrontation. He has figured out a way to meet their malicious intentions with mercy. From the ground where he bent in confusion, Jesus rises up in clarity, knowing exactly what he needs to do.

Jesus turns to face the crowd and replies, "Let anyone among you who is without sin be the first to throw a stone at her" (John 8:7b, NRSV). What a brilliant, disarming answer! Jesus knows very well that no one among the religious authorities or in the larger crowd is without sin. Yet he doesn't say so. He doesn't point an accusatory finger directly at anyone. Every person there is to determine whether or not they are without sin. They are to point their finger at no one but themselves.

Those gathered certainly weren't expecting this kind of a response. Is there anyone bold enough among the crowd to claim to be without sin? Anyone who makes such a claim risks being seen by someone in the crowd who knows very well the sins of the person claiming to be sinless. And this person could easily point a finger and expose to the entire assembly the precise nature of these sins.

After stunning them with his response and awaiting theirs, Jesus bends down again and continues writing in the sand. This act of writing appears even more curious than the first. He has just given them his verbal reply to their question. Why, then, does he continue to write upon the ground?

Bending down a second time places Jesus in a prayerful posture once again. He has just given a nonviolent invitation to the crowd, a gesture that challenges each person there. He hopes that someone might have the courage to meet his invitation with a nonviolent response. But he has no idea what they will do. And so he humbly bends once again, as if in prayerful vigil, as he awaits their reply.

Jesus is also modeling the behavior he desires from each of them. Just as he bent toward God and his deepest self, he calls them to bend as well. He is calling them to bend away from the act of stoning allowed by law. He invites them to lean into humility and mercy by looking into their own hearts. He beckons them toward God and their deepest selves to ponder how to rise up in faithful response.

Those in the crowd who bend in spirit begin to see things differently. From this vantage point, hearts begin to soften as people realize that sin is a common thread linking them with the accused woman. The sins of one may be different from the sins of another, but they are all sins. Those who bend recognize that casting a stone at this woman would be like casting a stone at a mirror image of themselves. The mirror will shatter in shards upon the ground. Nothing will be healed by the action. And more will be broken.

"When they heard it," writes John, "they went away, one by one, beginning with the elders; and Jesus was left alone with the woman standing before him" (John 8:9, NRSV). At first glance, the choice of every person dropping their stones and walking away may appear unimportant. It may even appear cowardly, as if they don't have the courage to throw a stone. But if we look more deeply, we discover that their actions are extremely courageous. By walking away, each member of the crowd quietly challenges the authority of the scribes and Pharisees. They confront a law rooted in retribution and affirm an action rooted in compassion. Each of them seizes the nonviolent moment and makes a bold move on behalf of mercy.

When they listen to Jesus with the ear of their heart, they walk away. The elders among them, they who are probably respected in the community, make the first move. These wise ones are not without sin, will not claim to be, and will not cast a stone. It is a courageous move by respected members of the community and a risky one as well. The elders risk rejection by others in the crowd. They risk looking like fools and being considered cowards by those who may be inclined to stone the woman. They may also be branded as sympathetic to Jesus and supportive of his unconventional handling of this situation.

Despite all that is at risk, the gamble taken by the elders works. The nonviolent movement in the heart and feet of the first person inspires nonviolent movement in the heart and feet of the second. And the third. And the fourth. And on and on, as if a chain reaction of nonviolence has been set in motion. One by one they seize the moment at hand. The dynamic within the encounter shifts away from potential violence. And the nonviolent momentum grows, carrying the accused woman out of the danger zone and into the hands of mercy. For one brief and beautiful moment, the crowd beholds the change that can happen when we give ourselves to mercy.

The crowd could have easily followed the law that allowed the woman to be stoned and walked away with the pain of social transgression upon their hearts. Instead, they risk nonviolence and walk away with the glow of social transformation upon their hearts.

Each person who chooses to step away from the encounter without casting a stone walks away, at least for a moment, from a system that confuses justice with retribution. They step into an understanding of justice partnered with mercy. They widen the space for God's mercy in their hearts. And they create a space for mercy in their community where none existed before.

Jesus has gone beyond what he needed to do to widen the space for God's mercy in this encounter. This situation calls him to find a way that will allow the woman to go free. Yet he goes even further, reaching beyond the accused woman and into the heart of every person in his midst. Everyone there now knows what it is like to disarm a confrontation without resorting to violence. Each person now feels the touch of nonviolent transformation upon their soul. And they go forth bearing witness to the transfiguration that has happened in their midst.

The transformation that takes place in this story is the transformation that is possible through nonviolence. It is deep and authentic, and it reaches the furthest recesses of the human heart. It nudges us to view a confrontation by peering into a looking glass where we see the transgressions of another placed alongside our own misdeeds. We are reminded of our shared humanity, our common failures, and our collective desire for wholeness. We come to realize that we are all sisters and brothers in one human family, accomplishing much, blundering often, in need of God's mercy at every turn.

As this Gospel story reaches its end, only Jesus and the accused woman remain. Jesus foiled the plan of the religious leaders by outwitting them. He utterly transformed the situation by drawing the entire crowd into the wideness of God's mercy. Left alone with the woman, Jesus asks, "Woman, where are they? Has no one condemned you?" She replies, "No one, sir." Yet she doesn't know what Jesus will do now that they are alone. Jesus reaches into her uncertainty with words tender and forgiving, saying, "Neither do I condemn you. Go your way, and from now on do not sin again" (John 8:10–11, NRSV).

These words of Jesus reveal a hint of irony woven into this story. Jesus called upon the one without sin to cast the first stone. Who in the midst of the crowd is without sin? Jesus alone. Only he could have honestly bent down, picked up a stone, and thrown it at the woman. Yet he who could have cast a stone instead casts the woman into the outstretched arms of mercy and forgiveness. By doing so, Jesus reinforces the notion that nonviolence is about conversion rather than condemnation.

While it is unlikely that any of us will find ourselves in a situation quite like this, there are elements of this story that resonate deeply with our everyday experience. Like finding ourselves catapulted into a confrontation not of our choosing with no warning and for which we feel entirely unprepared. Or finding ourselves in a situation where we feel outnumbered, unequal in power, or in some way at a disadvantage. Or facing a confrontation where we feel pushed into an either/or corner, not wanting to choose any of the options placed on the table. Or struggling with an encounter where we feel pressured to respond right away before things get out of control or someone gets hurt.

Sound familiar? Confrontations that happen without warning are often the times we find it hardest to seize the nonviolent moment. They catch us off guard, and we can easily get caught up in the swirling dynamics of the confrontation. When we find ourselves facing a confrontation, whether with a person, a group, or even an entire social system, we face a nonviolent moment. We can allow the negative momentum to escalate, a choice that is certain to lead to more pain and greater division. Or we can break the negative momentum of the conflict by following the lessons contained in this Gospel story.

We begin as Jesus did, by standing our ground. This term has taken on a very specific social meaning since the 2013 trial of George Zimmerman for the killing of Trayvon Martin. Mr. Zimmerman was found innocent according to the Florida law referred to as "Stand Your Ground." This law makes it legal for a person who feels threatened in a confrontation to use lethal force without requiring that the person first try to retreat. Acting in this way goes against everything that Jesus does when he stands his ground in this Gospel story. He shows us that standing your ground within a Christian spirituality of nonviolence looks entirely different from standing your ground in a culture of violence.

Acting like Jesus in this story can be hard work, and for many of us it's the more difficult and courageous choice when confrontation suddenly arises. It's hard to remain rooted. It's difficult to keep our cool. It may be much easier to let ourselves become unraveled, to be plucked out of our spiritual center and into the lion's den of our own anger or that of the powers standing on the other side of the confrontation. For some of us, it may be easier to give in to those who initiate the conflict. It may be safer to just smile and squelch the anger and pain we feel within.

When we stand our ground in a Christian context, we refuse to allow ourselves to be manipulated or coerced by others in the conflict. Like Jesus in this story, we humbly yet firmly refuse to allow the actions of others to dictate our response. We cannot control the actions of others. But we can choose our own actions and determine our response. We can be true to ourselves and to our Christian identity, remembering that the way we act will have an impact on the outcome of the confrontation. We have a measure of power in this situation, a power that can do harm or good. The only way our impact will be nonviolent is if we choose the power of nonviolence.

Standing our ground while remaining true to nonviolence also means not doing several things. We refuse to let our anger get the best of us. We don't put up invisible walls or assume a defensive posture. We don't become haughty. And we don't use violence when we feel threatened. To the best of our ability, we don't do anything that would make us a barrier in the conflict rather than a byway of the conflict's resolution. When we stand our ground, we do so holding steadfast to our nonviolent morals and principles and holding just as firmly to humility and respect, both for others and for ourselves.

Even as we stand our ground, we maintain a posture of openness. This is a very countercultural thing to do. In so many ways, society teaches us to approach those on the other side of a conflict with a staunch exterior, showing no signs of openness. We are told we must be strong and tough. We must take the upper hand. We must defend ourselves and our turf at all costs. We must not expose ourselves in any way to our opponent, as if hiding behind a mighty mask will somehow influence the situation in a positive way.

Nonviolence invites both parties in a conflict or people on opposing sides of an issue to approach one another in a posture of utter openness. We open ourselves to those on the other side of the conflict or issue, even though anger might be swelling within us. We remain open to the myriad number of ways the conflict or issue might be transformed. And we remain open to the creative power of nonviolence flowing within us, enticing us toward new and as yet undiscovered ways of moving forward. We ask ourselves, "Will the next thing I say or do help the situation or hinder it?"

Once we gain a foothold in the confrontation by standing our ground, the next move we must make is to step back. Just as Jesus did, we step back from the whirlwinds gaining speed within us and around us. There is a Haitian proverb that says, "We see from where we stand." When we stand in the midst of tumult, our vision is obstructed by tumult. When we step back, we step into a fresh perspective that gives us some distance from the confrontation. We create the space we need to assess the situation, take stock of our resources, consider possible options, and determine our response.

Sometimes we will step back from the confrontation in a literal and physical way. But even when there seems to be no space to step back in body, we can always step back in spirit. We step back into our spiritual center where God makes haste to help us. We gather up our pieces that are becoming unglued and place them before God, who puts us back together. Within the harbor of our spiritual center, we start to see and think more clearly. We breathe deeply, and the breath of God's spirit rises up in us, bringing a measure of calm. We remember that the armor we wear in this conflict is the mantle of God's love, a love that shelters us through every exposed minute of the encounter.

As we begin to regain our composure, we are ready to take another step. And our next step is to bend. Like Jesus, we bend in spirit toward God and our deepest selves, asking, "How in God's name will I respond to this?" We bend away from hostility toward humility. We ask God to show us the way through this conflict. We go to the deep place within where we are rooted in God. The roots of God's love stretch far and wide into the sands of our soul. And these roots will steady us through this encounter.

After bending, we rise up and do what we can to transform the situation at hand. We do our best to remain calm and centered. We draw upon resources like surprise and creativity. We may do something entirely unexpected to diffuse the tension and open up new possibilities for moving forward. We choose our words carefully, as Jesus did, using language that invites rather than indicts. We extend an invitation to all involved to search their hearts as they ponder what to do next. We open up a space for mercy as we try to guide the conflict toward a just and peaceful resolution.

Sometimes our efforts will succeed. At other times they won't. Nonviolent actions do not guarantee a nonviolent outcome. But the only way to work toward a nonviolent resolution is by giving nonviolence a chance. We may find that we try to negotiate a conflict in this way but in the midst of it we become unraveled and end up doing or saying something we regret. If so, the invitation is not to abandon the course we've begun. Rather, we take some time to collect ourselves and try to resolve the conflict using these steps at another time.

We follow the example of Jesus, who challenges condemnation with mercy. Jesus urges the crowd not to condemn the accused woman. He urges them to turn away from cruelty toward compassion. As they do, they begin a process that will continue long after this encounter. They will reflect upon the transformation they helped bring about. They may think about the fact that they chose the law of love over the law of the land. They may consider what this act of mercy means in the context of their lives and how it may be a step toward further growth in the future.

The power of this Gospel story becomes even greater when we consider the actions of Jesus in a social context. In a patient yet purposeful way, Jesus stood up to a system of legalized brutality. He challenged a law that sanctioned death as a fitting punishment for a serious sin. He refused to abide by the prevailing notion that "doing justice" meant death by stoning. He put forth instead an understanding of justice that was interwoven with mercy.

By standing up to the law that allowed the woman to be stoned, Jesus stands up to the notion that justice can somehow be partnered with retribution. This type of "justice" violated everything that Jesus knew to be true. The justice that Jesus knew and lived day after day was a justice that partners again and again with mercy. This justice shares nothing in common with vengeance. It is a justice that breaks the cycle of violence and draws a wounded world into the wideness of God's mercy.

Jesus stood up to vengeance masquerading as justice in his day, and his strength and spirit can be heard in the words of the US Catholic bishops in our day:

> We are tragically turning to violence in the search for quick and easy answers to complex human problems. A society which . . . relies on vengeance fails fundamental moral tests. . . .
> We cannot teach that killing is wrong by killing.[2]

The call to mercy issued by Jesus and repeated by the bishops rings out urgently in a world well-versed in vengeance. Over time, the stones that harden our hearts and undergird social policies have grown in size and scope. Stones of fear, prejudice, and hatred are carried in the hearts of too many individuals, communities, and countries. Stones of retribution increasingly find their way into our legal system, evidenced by the Stand Your Ground laws that have passed in several states. Our nation has become the world's unrivaled Goliath, harboring more military stones than the rest of the world's Davids combined. And nuclear stones, hoarded by countries with stockpiles and highly desired by countries without, are forming the foundation of a new and more volatile nuclear age.

Amid such a stony climate, we must ask ourselves some soul-searching questions. Will we join with society in casting stones of hubris, greed ,and hatred at others? Or will we lay down our stones and challenge others to do the same? Will we be complicit with a society that legalizes violence and equates "getting justice" with "getting even"? Or will we raise our voices to advance an understanding of justice partnered with mercy? Will we wait for someone else to mount a compassionate challenge to the stone-hearted policies and practices of society? Or will we risk the nonviolent way and be an example for others to follow?

As we discern our answers to these questions, the example of the elders in this Gospel story gives us all the guidance we need.

We are called to lead society away from our modern stone age toward the empathic era when our strength will be measured by the wideness of our mercy. We must challenge the prevailing belief that "getting justice" means "getting even" by cultivating a justice that makes room for mercy. We must call our society to lay down every stone intent upon destruction

2. US Conference of Catholic Bishops, *Confronting a Culture of Violence*, Section II, "A Culture of Violence."

to form the constructs of a world intent upon compassion. "Our faith challenges each of us to examine how we can contribute to an ethic which . . . values kindness and compassion over anger and vengeance," wrote the US Catholic bishops. "A growing sense of national fear and failure must be replaced by a new commitment to solidarity and the common good."[3]

As we go about this work, let us remember the power that stirred the crowd in this Gospel story as they walked together toward a new way of being. It began with the simple choice of the elders. Simply and nonviolently, the wise elders walked away, and this choice inspired nonviolence in the hearts of others in the crowd. Together they walked away, quietly renouncing violence as they calmly chose nonviolence. They propelled the nonviolent moment into a landslide of nonviolent momentum. And this momentum carried the moment, sparing the life of the accused woman.

This momentum is being felt today in any number of places in our nation and around the world. I've been especially heartened by the outpouring of those who are standing up for mercy around the nation in an effort to repeal Stand Your Ground laws. These people are following in the footsteps of Jesus and the crowd in this Gospel story by standing up to laws that legalize vengeance. Members of the Christian community are boldly proclaiming that these kinds of laws contradict the teachings of Jesus. People are being called to search their hearts, like the crowd in this story, to decide whether to support such laws or join with those who are walking together toward a vision of justice that makes room for mercy.

Never underestimate the power of a nonviolent choice to influence the actions of others. When we choose nonviolence as individuals, others may be inspired to follow our lead. When we choose nonviolence as a community, we can create a momentum that is truly transformational. We become a people walking steadily and courageously toward the peaceful world we desire. With each step we take, the momentum builds. It is the momentum that flows from a mercy that is wider than the sea, expanding outward to the furthest reaches of the horizon.

When we give ourselves to this flow of mercy and become vessels of it, the toughened places of our world become a little more tender. The callous ways of society become a little more compassionate. And the wideness of God's mercy stretches a little further into a narrow-hearted world.

3. Ibid., Section II, "A Culture of Violence."

Questions for Reflection and Conversation

1. In this Gospel story, Jesus issues a nonviolent invitation to the crowd, and the crowd accepts it. Where is the nonviolent invitation in your life? What might it be inviting you to do or to become?

2. Think of a present or recent conflict in your life. Call to mind the posture that nonviolence calls us to take amidst a conflict—to stand our ground true to the ways of nonviolence, to step back and collect ourselves, to remain open, to bend toward humility. If you were to assume this nonviolent posture, how might it help you to resolve the conflict in mind?

3. When faced with a conflict, have you ever taken any of the steps outlined in this chapter? Have you used other nonviolent methods to disarm a conflict? What were the results?

4. What do you believe is the relationship between mercy and justice? How would you describe the relationship between mercy and justice portrayed in our society?

5. Jesus and those who walk away from this confrontation take a risk on behalf of nonviolence. What are you willing to risk for the sake of nonviolence?

6. Where in your heart and in your life is the wideness of God's mercy needed? What can you do to bring mercy into these areas?

6

Breaking the Chains that Bind

THE SPIRITUALITY OF NONVIOLENCE calls us to live in right relationship. This includes our relationship with God and ourselves as well as our relationships with one another and all creation. We are called to cultivate bonds of right relationship in a world of too many strained relationships. And we are invited to build the beloved community in a society that has more than its share of broken communities.

The concept of the beloved community was foundational to the work of the Rev. Dr. Martin Luther King Jr. In the beloved community, all people are treated with respect and dwell together in justice and peace. Dr. King believed that nonviolence was never to be engaged in for its own sake. Living in right relationship as members of the beloved community was the goal. Acting nonviolently in a spirit of right relationship was the means of achieving this goal.

Dr. King understood that nonviolence always seeks an end result greater than itself. "The end is reconciliation;" said Dr. King, "the end is redemption; the end is the creation of the beloved community."[1] The concept of beloved community may sound like a utopian idea, especially in this day and age of so much violence. Yet the work of nonviolence is about building this community little by little. Every nonviolent word and deed we engage in transforms the world we know into the world God desires. We break the chains that bind us together in wrong relationship and cultivate bonds that unite us in right relationship.

---

1. King, Speech.

There's a powerful Gospel story about a tormented person bound in wrong relationship that contains many lessons for living in right relationship. It's the story of Jesus healing a man possessed by a mighty demon named Legion. This story is one of several where Jesus uses his power to cast out a demon. Yet this particular story is about much more. It's about a community struggling to contend with a problem in its midst. The more the community struggles with this problem, the more it gets tangled up in a web of wrong relationship. As the story unfolds, it sheds light upon the steps we can take to untangle ourselves from this very same web.

The story takes place in Gerasa, a country in Gentile territory where Jesus has just arrived after a stormy night at sea. "And when he had stepped out of the boat," Scripture tells us, "immediately a man out of the tombs with an unclean spirit met him" (Mark 5:2, NRSV). The demon that has taken hold of this tormented person is so fearsome that members of the community had taken to shackling him. "No one could restrain him anymore, even with a chain," Scripture tells us, "for he had often been restrained with shackles and chains, but the chains he wrenched apart, and the shackles he broke in pieces" (Mark 5:3–4, NRSV).

This man with a demon is a striking symbol of someone bound by chains of wrong relationship and the suffering born of such struggle. Because of the demon, he is unable to live in right relationship with himself or anyone else. His life is one of constant chaos and despair. The demons have taken such a hold upon him that he makes his home among the dead. The situation is made even worse by the Gerasene people who chained him up like an animal. He is utterly bound, body and soul.

Take a moment now to consider the Gerasene community. The people are faced with the problem of a person possessed by a demon. They fear for their safety. They want to do something to protect themselves from the man's insane behavior. They may also want to protect him from harming himself because of the demon. So they shackle this beleaguered soul again and again. When he breaks through the chains, they try new means of restraint, hoping that bigger and better chains will be able to hold him bound.

But no matter how hard the Gerasene people try to restrain him, they do not succeed. "And no one had the strength to subdue him," Scripture tells us (Mark 5:4, NRSV). No matter what method of restraint they tried, no matter who tried it or how many, they failed. No one and nothing was powerful enough.

This troubled person and the Gerasene community offer a striking example of what it means to live in wrong relationship. Because of the demon, the man cannot cultivate right relationships with anyone, including himself. Because of the demon, the community is binding someone who is already bound. They are placing external chains upon a person who is already fettered interiorly. Each time they place another chain upon him, they place another chain around their community. They become more bound, not less. And they come no closer to liberating themselves from the unwelcome demon in their midst.

From the moment Jesus encounters this tormented person, his way of dealing with the situation is entirely different. He makes no attempt to subdue him or the spirits that hold him bound. Instead, he approaches the situation with openness and great compassion. Jesus understands that this person's liberation is linked with the liberation of the troubled community. Neither he nor the Gerasene people can be free until they no longer have to contend with the demon dwelling in their midst.

After the man with a demon runs up to Jesus and falls in worship before him, the demon says, "What have you to do with me, Jesus, Son of the Most High God? I adjure you by God, do not torment me" (Mark 5:7, NRSV). Jesus has not uttered a word about himself and is in Gentile territory. Yet this demon knows exactly who he is. We then learn that Jesus had already tried to cast out the demon. At some point before the demon speaks, Jesus had said, "Come out of the man, you unclean spirit!"(Mark 5:8, NRSV). But his efforts had failed.

Perhaps this is because the demon has the upper hand at this point in the encounter. The demon knows who Jesus is and obviously knows something about what Jesus is capable of doing, and with this knowledge comes power. Yet Jesus remains in the dark about the identity of this particular demon. He needs to learn more in order to cast it out.

So Jesus asks the demon, "What is your name?" (Mark 5:9, NRSV). This simple question is the key that begins to unlock the chains binding this community. Rather than trying to fetter this ferocious spirit, Jesus faces it directly. "My name is Legion," the demon replies, "for we are many" (Mark 5:9, NRSV). The enormity of what Jesus is contending with suddenly becomes clear. He's not dealing with just one demon—he's dealing with a whole host of them! It's no wonder he couldn't cast out this demon the first time he tried. He is up against a large squadron that requires something very different.

As soon as Legion reveals its name, the balance of power in this story shifts. Jesus now knows what he is dealing with and with this knowledge comes power. Now that Legion's identity is known the demons discover they are powerless and their clenches are weakened. Legion begs Jesus not to be sent out of the country and pleads to be sent into a nearby herd of swine instead. "And the unclean spirits came out and entered the swine;" Mark writes, "and the herd, numbering about two thousand, rushed down the steep bank into the lake, and were drowned in the lake" (Mark 5:13, NRSV).

At long last, Jesus has removed the unwelcome demons from this place where they have been dwelling for too long. He has broken the chains binding this individual and the Gerasene community. The man is now free to live a normal life. And the members of the community are free to live their lives without a demon lurking in their midst.

What are we to make of this story as we explore the spirituality of nonviolence? And what meaning does the demon Legion hold for us today? *Legion* is a term used to mean "many." Historically it referred to a division of the Roman army that could number as many as five or six thousand men.[2] The enormity of this demon invites us to consider this story on a much larger scale. If we look closely we find that it contains important lessons for communities trying to deal with a host of problems in their midst.

I see Legion as a symbol of the multitude of demons plaguing our world today. By "demons" I mean the social problems that trouble the times in which we live. Like the problems of homelessness and undocumented immigration or the much larger problems of terrorism and racism, to name just a few. The community and its leaders, whether local, national, or global, must figure out how to respond to these problems. More often than not, we respond like the Gerasene community. We take steps to protect ourselves from the problem and the people associated with it. In the process, we place chains around our hearts, chains that bind us together in wrong relationship. And we do nothing to resolve the problem in a lasting way.

This behavior can be seen in the way we deal with many social problems. Cities force homeless people out of public areas in an effort to increase safety and improve public image. We construct walls and create legal barriers to prevent immigrants from enjoying the freedoms we take for granted. People suspected of links to terrorism are rounded up, imprisoned, held in legal limbo, and even tortured. We conduct military campaigns in countries

2. *The Interpreter's Dictionary of the Bible, K–Q,* 110.

believed to harbor terrorists with blatant disregard for the damage we are inflicting upon innocent people in the process.

Each of these responses to a particular social problem uses what I call the "chain approach." This approach does one of two things. It either constructs barriers between communities and the problems in their midst, or it seeks to apprehend or harm people associated with the problem. Each time we use this approach, we place another chain upon a world already bound by too much fear and mistrust. We place another chain around our hearts, making us an increasingly hard-hearted people. And we add another chain to the thousands already binding our world in a tangled web of wrong relationship.

Once we begin binding ourselves up in this way, we have a tendency to continue. It's like the Gerasene community placing chain after chain upon the demented man. They kept trying new chains even though the man kept breaking through every chain they placed upon him. When we try to bind up the demons in our midst, we set in motion a momentum that becomes difficult to stop. We lock ourselves into a pattern of behavior and become tangled up in the process. Once we're tangled, it becomes hard to figure out how to break free from the morass in which we are embroiled.

Take for example the way our nation approaches national defense. We try to contain threats to our national security by devoting more than a half trillion tax dollars to military spending each year. We have spent more than $7.6 trillion on defense and homeland security since September 11, 2001.[3] We have become the world's unrivaled superpower, with a military budget that dwarfs the defense spending of other nations. In the process of building such an expansive military system, our nation's moral compass has come to resemble a military compass. Instead of breaking the chains that bind our world in wrong relationship, we bolster them with military might. And we become tangled up with the very demons we are trying to restrain.

Our nation sells weapons to countries in an effort to make our world safer. We then spend billions of dollars to produce bigger and better weapons to protect ourselves from the weapons we just sold. Our national leaders try to force dictatorial leaders of other nations to respect human rights by dropping indiscriminate bombs that slaughter human beings along with human rights. We try to prevent future terrorist attacks by terrorizing people through sweeping military campaigns in other nations. We

---

3. The National Priorities Project, *Military Spending in Fiscal Year 2013 and Beyond* and *U.S. Security Spending Since 9/11.*

use weapons that inflict massive destruction to attack a nation suspected of having weapons of mass destruction (Iraq) to purportedly protect the world from weapons of mass destruction.

Round and round it goes. Where it ends, God alone knows. Our nation, which claims to be the land of the free, has become the land of the fettered. We have become bound up with the very demons we are trying to restrain. And we are increasingly binding our world in a tangled web of wrong relationship.

No one had the strength to subdue Legion in the Gerasene community long ago. And no one has the strength to subdue the social demons that are legion in the global community today. No method of restraint, no matter how well-orchestrated, will succeed. Every effort to subdue, even the most sophisticated, will fail. Why? Because a world where all dwell with one another in right relationship cannot be built through efforts that bind us in wrong relationship. Liberation from the demons in our midst comes about not through chains but through change. "[O]ur society needs a moral revolution to replace a culture of violence with a renewed ethic of justice, responsibility and community," wrote the US Catholic bishops. "God's wisdom, love and commandments can show us the way to live, heal and reconcile."[4]

Jesus modeled this kind of moral revolution for the Gerasene people long ago. When he came to Gerasa, he had no intention of further binding this already bound community. He broke the cycle of violence that was wreaking havoc on the Gerasene man and community. In the process, he invited us into a revolutionary way of contending with people and problems in our midst.

Jesus seized the nonviolent moment by first separating the problem from the person. It's important to note that all of the dialogue up to the point where Jesus drives Legion out of the man takes place between Jesus and Legion. Jesus knows that his full attention must be directed toward the demon that is doing the tormenting.

This is an important lesson for us to remember when we find ourselves contending with social demons. We must learn to separate the problems plaguing society from the people affected by these problems. Too often our society treats those affected by a problem as if they *are* the problem. This places more chains upon people already bound in some way. It does

---

4. US Conference of Catholic Bishops, *Confronting a Culture of Violence*, Section II "A Culture of Violence."

nothing to resolve the problem at hand because it never gets to the root of the problem. And too often it leads to demonizing people already struggling with demons of their own.

A few years ago, leaders in the city where I live decided that panhandlers were becoming a nuisance. Their presence was not helping our city's image and they made the downtown area a less desirable place to live and work. A publicity campaign was initiated in an effort to address the problem. Billboards were placed around the community that read, "Panhandling is not the solution—give to local charities." Maybe if these undesirable people don't get the handouts they're looking for, they thought, they'll go elsewhere.

In the end, this campaign didn't work. The panhandlers didn't go away. Why? Because panhandlers were treated as if they were the problem when the real problem needing to be addressed was poverty. Panhandlers, already considered outcasts by many, were further rejected. People who might normally consider giving to them became conflicted about what was the "right" thing to do. Chains were placed around the heart of our community, and we became more bound, not less.

Separating the problem from the person involves naming and facing our demons. In the dialogue between Jesus and Legion, the pivotal moment arrives when Jesus learns the demon's name. Jesus now understands the nature of the problem tormenting the man. He draws into the light the evil spirits that shore up their power in darkness. The power of the demons begins to recede. And Jesus finds what he needs to anchor himself for the work of liberation.

Naming the forces that bind a person, a community, or a society is a crucial step in breaking the chains that hold us bound. When these forces lurking in the shadows are brought into the light, we discover what we are dealing with. Once we've named the problem at hand, we can take steps to contend with it. And with each step we take, power flows out of the hold of the demons and into the hands of nonviolence.

Our nation has a powerful example of people who named a social demon and contended with it using the power of nonviolence. The civil rights movement named the social demon of racism and exposed the evil of segregation. The courageous people who formed this movement knew that racism was binding people together in wrong relationship. They understood that they must do something that would break rather than bolster these chains. And so they faced this demon head on.

They called this demon by its true name each time they identified institutions and social structures bound by the clenches of racism. Segregated schools, restaurants, and other public facilities were named. Public transportation, employment, and the voting system were named. Through a massive media campaign, proponents of civil rights drew racism out of the shadows and into the national spotlight. Their brave and pioneering efforts sent shock waves rippling across our nation. No longer could we deny the social demon in our midst. No longer could we deny the hideous hold of this demon on our hearts. Their nonviolent campaign awakened an entire nation to the evil of racial discrimination gripping the South with a hold that had no intention of letting go.

As the face of racism was revealed, nonviolence gained the foothold it needed. Like Jesus facing the demon directly, this movement confronted segregation directly through nonviolent campaigns for the common good. In Montgomery, people took to the streets in a massive bus boycott that moved the public transportation system toward integration. In Birmingham, people of color were beaten and jailed simply for sitting down at segregated lunch counters. They opened the door of integration in restaurants and public facilities through their nonviolent protests. In Selma, thousands of people, both black and white, took to the streets, marching together toward the day when African Americans could vote freely and without fear of intimidation.

The civil rights movement reconfigured the face of the nation, particularly the South. The movement revealed the power of nonviolence as it had never been revealed before in the history of this nation. It broke chains that were binding communities and opened many a closed mind. And it proved that masses of people empowered by nonviolence and united by a common goal can effectively contend with a demon as entrenched as racism.

Of course the civil rights movement did not entirely liberate society from the grip of racism. Like Legion, racism is an entrenched demon that lives deep within the marrow of our nation. But this movement made great strides toward liberation. It dragged an ugly and insidious demon into the light and called it by its true name. It created a foundation upon which hundreds of thousands of people have stood since, utilizing nonviolence to continue the slow yet steady work of liberation. And it pioneered the pathway that led to the election of the first African American president in the history of our nation.

What the civil rights movement accomplished was truly extraordinary. And the way this movement accomplished it was just as extraordinary. For the leaders of this movement, living in right relationship was not only their goal. It was also the means of achieving that goal.

Those who participated in the nonviolent campaigns of the civil rights movement did so in a spirit of right relationship. Their actions targeted unjust laws rather than unjust people. They did not shout at those who threw racial slurs and barbs at them. They did not retaliate or use oppressive means to counter the violence they faced. Instead, they put into action a love strong enough to embrace even enemies as beloved. "With every ounce of our energy," wrote Dr. King, "we must continue to rid this nation of the incubus of segregation. But we shall not in the process relinquish our privilege and our obligation to love. While abhorring segregation, we shall love the segregationist. This is the only way to create the beloved community."[5]

The privilege and obligation to love even those who oppress us is an important aspect of how nonviolence slowly builds the beloved community. The words of one civil rights protester who experienced physical abuse for his participation in the lunch counter sit-ins speak volumes about the lengths that nonviolence will go to foster a spirit of right relationship. "I will let them kick me and kick me," he said, "until they have kicked all hatred out of themselves and into my own body where I will transform it into love."[6]

It may be extremely difficult for us to imagine ever acting as this man did. How hard it is to think about meeting eyes of hatred with eyes of love! But this man understood that those who were kicking him were not the problem. The problem was a pervasive racism that bound him up with them in chains of wrong relationship. These chains caused people to kick him. These chains subjected him to maltreatment because of the color of his skin. Neither of them would be free until these chains of racism were broken.

All who participated in the civil rights movement decided to do their part in breaking these chains by receiving the violence targeted toward them in a spirit of love. As hard as this can be, we are called to do the same. Jesus made this crystal clear, saying, "You have heard it said, 'Love your neighbor—but hate your enemy.' But I tell you, love your enemies and pray

5. King, "Loving Your Enemies," 54.

6. Kownacki, *Love Beyond Measure*, 7.

for your persecutors. This will prove that you are children of God" (Matt 5:43–45a, TIB). Jesus tells us we are to build bonds of right relationship even with our enemies. And when we do, we foster right relationship with our God.

It may take awhile to get to the point of being able to love our enemies. But we strive to answer the call by following in the footsteps of those who show us the way. If I am treated wrongly, I can act rightly. I can hold fast to my vision of the beloved community even as I experience the blows of a broken community. I can seek to transform the hurt of wrong relationship by drawing it into the heart of right relationship. Why? Because right relationship cannot be cultivated through attitudes and actions of wrong relationship. The beloved community can only be created when we break, rather than bolster, the chains that bind our hearts. None of us will be free until all of us are free.

This is the challenge and the invitation placed before us by Jesus. And it is the same challenge and invitation that Jesus placed before the Gerasene community after liberating them from the demon of Legion.

This Gospel story doesn't end when Jesus drives out the demons. Mark writes, "The man who had been possessed by demons begged him that he might be with him" (Mark 5:18, NRSV). Like others in Scripture, the one who is healed longs to remain with Jesus. And in this case, he may very well long to leave this place that has caused him such pain. But Jesus doesn't grant his request. "Go home to your people," Jesus tells him, "and tell them what our God has done for you" (Mark 5:19, TIB). Restored to right relationship within his being, this man is returned home to cultivate right relationship within the Gerasene community.

And there is a great deal of work to be done there. The members of the community are confused and frightened by all that has taken place in such a short time. Jesus has created an opportunity for the community to cultivate right relationship. But it will be up to them to determine whether they seize or squander the nonviolent moment before them. How will they treat the person they once treated as an outcast? How will they be treated in return? And how will all that has happened impact them as a community?

"He went away and began to proclaim in the Decapolis how much Jesus had done for him," writes Mark (Mark 5:20, NRSV). This liberated person is sent forth as an ambassador of right relationship. He is to bestow upon members of the community the same mercy Jesus bestowed upon him. Each time he meets someone who glared at him with eyes of condemnation, he is to gaze upon them with eyes of compassion. Whenever he encounters someone who placed a chain upon him, he is to reach through the pain of what has been toward the promise of what can be. He is to touch the fearful hearts of those who treated him as an outcast with the love showered upon him by Jesus, a love that excludes no one.

This Scripture story draws to a close by telling us that "everyone was amazed" by the actions of the liberated person (Mark 5:20b, NRSV). We will never know exactly what took place. But we know that the hearts of the Gerasene people were in awe of what was happening in their midst. And we can believe that the liberated man was doing his part to transform his broken community into a beloved community.

Maybe Scripture leaves this story somewhat open-ended because the ending is up to us. This story is our story, the story of a people bound together in wrong relationship, yearning for the grace of right relationship. Can we break the chains that bind us and embrace the change that can set us free? Will we help build the beloved community by reaching out to those with whom we live in broken community?

Speaking of the spirit of the beloved community, Dr. King once said, "It is this type of spirit and this type of love that can transform opposers into friends. It is this type of understanding goodwill that will transform the deep gloom of the old age into the exuberant gladness of the new age. It is this love which will bring about miracles . . . ".[7] Miracles like the love that broke the chains binding the Gerasene community long ago. And miracles like the love that can break the chains binding the global community today.

Questions for Reflection and Conversation

1. What does the term "beloved community" mean to you? What kinds of behaviors would characterize a beloved community?

2. What does it mean for you to live in right relationship with God and yourself? With others? With all creation?

3. Have you ever treated a person as if they were a problem rather than separating the problem from the person? What was the end result?

4. Where do the chains of wrong relationship exist in your life? Where do these chains exist in society? What steps can you/we take to break the chains that bind and cultivate bonds of right relationship?

7. King, Speech.

5. Consider a particular social problem plaguing society today. What are some of the underlying factors that contribute to the existence of this problem? How can we use nonviolence to address this problem?

6. How do you respond to the call of Jesus to "love your enemies and pray for those who persecute you"? Who or what do you regard as enemy? What steps can you take to lead you toward following this command when it seems too difficult?

7

Nonviolence and the Call to Conversion

THE CALL OF NONVIOLENCE in our lives is an ongoing call to conversion. This conversion begins in the hearts of each of us and reaches out to the heart of society. The more we learn about the spirituality of nonviolence, the more we become aware of those places in our lives in need of transformation. This is why turning toward nonviolence is not a one-time event but something that happens repeatedly. It is an act of tilling our inner seedbed over and over and tending to our spiritual soil so that new growth will sprout.

When I think about individuals in Scripture who embody the call to conversion, the first person who comes to mind is John the Baptist. His way of life was stark, his preaching prophetic, and his commitment to his call unfailing. John focused on the conversion of hearts and minds and challenged all who came to him to change their ways. He emphasized the essential role of repentance in leading a life of faithfulness. He lived on the margins of society, drawn deep into the wilderness of God's way. John made his dwelling place on the border region of faith between the world as he knew it and the world as God desires it to be.

"He went into all the region around the Jordan," Scripture tells us, "proclaiming a baptism of repentance for the forgiveness of sins" (Luke 3:3, NRSV). He called to repentance those whose hearts had gone astray and those whose feet were in step with a wayward society. Those who entered into John's baptism entered into a new way of being. They gave God their hearts of stone and God gave them hearts of flesh in return.

Each time we realize we've committed some kind of transgression, we face a nonviolent moment. And the way we seize it is through repentance. Repentance is a step toward an authentic change of heart, moving us from wrongful behavior toward right relationship. It is also a turning point. We turn toward our remorse and it becomes our catalyst for conversion. We turn toward God, who receives our prodigal hearts with open arms of love and forgiveness. And we turn toward our sincere desire to not repeat whatever it is we've done wrong.

This act of turning is an act of humility. When we come face-to-face with our transgressions, we are invited to admit them with honesty and integrity. Repentance clothes our souls in sackcloth as we reveal our shortcomings before God and take responsibility for our failings. This act of humility grounds us in our humanity. We remember that we are not God, but mere mortals who make mistakes and repeatedly need to seek God's forgiveness. Yet even our trespasses can be a point of connection for us, not only to God but to one another. I am broken through the wrongs I do. You are broken through the wrongs you do. And in this brokenness we share common ground.

Repentance plays an important role within the spirituality of nonviolence, especially when situated in a society that is increasingly unrepentant. The daily news is filled with stories about people engaged in immoral acts who seem to have no qualms about their behavior (until they are caught). Leaders in our nation and around the globe break laws with impunity, deeming their conduct necessary for the well-being of those they lead. Time after time, those who break the law plead "not guilty" rather than taking responsibility for their crimes. And how often do we see influential people claiming they don't remember saying or doing a certain something that was wrong? These actions send a message that it is acceptable to try to get away with misdeeds rather than admitting responsibility and facing the consequences of our actions.

Even our church at times is guilty of this type of behavior. I remember when news about the US clergy sex abuse scandal broke, sending shock waves through the Catholic church. At the meeting of the US Catholic bishops that followed, I longed to see a photo of the bishops together on their knees in a posture of repentance. I wanted those who were complicit with the abuse to accept responsibility and those who weren't to pray for the bishops and priests who were. Sadly, this never happened, at least not in a public way. In the years since, there have been individual bishops who have done their part to take responsibility. But many others have tried to seal documents and cover up the wrongdoing that took place.

These moral leaders have struggled to model repentance in a church where repentance is raised to the level of a sacrament. Their struggle reminds us how hard it can be to fully and freely repent of our sins. It reminds us that the tendency to hide our wrongdoings rather than taking responsibility for them is present in the church as well as in the larger society. And it reminds us that the need for repentance in these troubled times is great.

There is a longing in God's heart for us to turn away from our transgressions, whatever they may be, and turn with repentant hearts toward God. Like the father in the story of the prodigal one, God eagerly awaits our return and gazes off into the distance to catch sight of us as we make our way back. When we do, God's heart skips a beat. We are enfolded in arms of forgiveness that tenderly touch our remorseful souls. In this warm and loving embrace, our wrongdoing melts away. We are restored to the fold of right relationship with God and with ourselves. We have answered the call to conversion by coming home to God. And we are ready to try again.

The spirituality of nonviolence invites us to cultivate a regular rhythm of repentance in our lives. We are called to come before God on a regular basis, admit our wrongdoings, and reflect upon these failures in the gentle light of God's love. In this way, we confess our ongoing need for God's mercy. We experience the grace of reconciliation and the gratitude that flows from it. And we bear witness to the need for continued conversion in our lives. When we are regularly reconciled with God in this way, we can engage in our work for nonviolence with a sense of honesty, humility, and integrity. As we do, we model how much repentance can offer to a society sorely in need of it.

The gifts that repentance offers are profound in and of themselves. Yet if we listen carefully to the message of John the Baptist, it becomes clear that repentance is the doorway to something more. After baptizing those who came to him, John said, "Bear fruits worthy of repentance" (Luke 3:8a, NRSV). It is not enough to experience the peace of God's pardon upon our souls. John tells us that a baptism of repentance calls for faith-filled action.

The crowds beg John to tell them what they must do to be bearers of good fruit. He instructs them accordingly, saying, "Whoever has two coats must share with anyone who has none; and whoever has food must do likewise" (Luke 3:11, NRSV). When the tax collectors find their way to him, he says, "Collect no more than the amount prescribed for you" (Luke

3:13, NRSV). And when soldiers arrive to hear him, he says, "Do not extort money from anyone by threats or false accusation, and be satisfied with your wages" (Luke 3:14b, NRSV).

In other words, do what is right in your lives and in your livelihoods. Act justly and practice humility. John acknowledges some of the injustices in society by pointing out that there are those who have enough and those who don't. There are those who are dishonest in their work and those who exploit others. John tells those inclined to act unjustly in their work to change their ways. But he also suggests that none of us is exempt from working for justice. All of us are called to transform society by doing our part to set things straight.

John suggests this when he tells those who have two coats to share with those who have none and those who have food to share with those who hunger. In this simple command, John is saying that all of us need to be concerned with the plight of those in need. All of us must awaken to the injustices that exist in our society and offer some response. All of us have a part to play in distributing the world's resources a little more equitably among the children of God. And all of us have a part to play in bringing a little more justice into the lives of others.

I remember my years working with impoverished immigrants in New York City, many of whom were undocumented. The challenges they faced in this nation were enormous. There were vast systems in place that were oppressing them in many ways. Yet each time they came to the community center where I worked, they were embraced with compassion and treated with the utmost dignity and respect. Treating them in a just manner had a tremendous impact on them. It boosted their self-confidence. It gave them positive energy to counter the negative influences in their lives. It helped some of them discover the inner strength they needed to move toward more self-sufficient lives. And it brought the spirit of justice into the lives of people swimming against a tide of injustice.

As the seeds of conversion take root in us and grow, the spirituality of nonviolence and its presence in our lives also grows. We foster mercy and understanding within our homes and our places of work and worship. We reach out with compassion to those in need in our communities. We negotiate our purchasing decisions with the nonnegotiable precepts of non-violence. We refine our lifestyle choices to reflect our growing respect for all creation. The specific ways we live out our commitment to nonviolence may differ. Yet these different manifestations flow from the same spirit.

And together they speak of the breadth of nonviolence and its potential for transforming our world.

The more the seeds of conversion sprout and take root in us, the more we become aware of our need for ongoing conversion. I remember once reading a story about Maya Angelou. She said that she often meets people who tell her enthusiastically that they are Christians. When they do she stops for a moment to think. She considers her age, her own spiritual journey, and how it has evolved over time. Then she looks at them and asks, "Already?" She went on to explain that we may strive to be Christian, but we are always on the way. Since we are constantly in a state of becoming it can be difficult to say that we've ever truly arrived.

Our relationship to the spirituality of nonviolence is similar. We strive to be people of nonviolence, yet we are constantly a work in progress. Can any of us ever truly say that we are nonviolent? We may act nonviolently in this situation or at that moment. We may work to build a strong foundation of nonviolence within our lives and in the life of our world. But if we are honest with ourselves, we will acknowledge those parts of our lives where nonviolence is still sorely needed. This truth is brought home to me anytime I get behind the wheel of a car. When I'm driving and someone does something that I deem to be wrong, a verbal tirade spills out of my mouth and nonviolence flies right out the window.

Moments like these are humbling reminders of our need for God's grace every step of the way. Each time we turn away from nonviolence we are given an opportunity to turn toward it yet again. We seize the nonviolent moment by giving nonviolence another chance to do its work in us. We acknowledge our mistakes, repent of our wrongdoings, and turn ourselves anew toward God. We circle around again, like clay spinning round and round upon the Potter's wheel. The touch of the Potter gently reworks our clay. And we are fashioned once again into a new creation.

The more we answer the call to conversion in our own lives, the more we become aware of the need for conversion in our society. This kind of conversion is exactly what the US Catholic bishops called for in their pastoral message on violence. "[C]ommitment and conversion can change us," they wrote, "and together we can change our culture and communities. Person by person, family by family, neighborhood by neighborhood, we must take our communities back from the evil and fear that come with so much violence."[1]

1. US Conference of Catholic Bishops, *Confronting a Culture of Violence*, Section I, "Introduction."

There is a crying need in this day and age for disciples willing to commit themselves to this kind of conversion. And there is a powerful Scripture story that speaks of just how far God will go to bring disciples to places where conversion is needed.

The Scripture I'm referring to is the story of God calling forth the prophet Jonah. I love this story because it is a tug-of-war between God's determination to send Jonah forth and Jonah's reluctance to go. And in this tug-of-war there is room for all of us who may harbor doubts and fears when we wrestle with God's call to conversion in our lives.

The story begins as God says to Jonah, "Go at once to Nineveh, that great city, and cry out against it, for their wickedness has come up before me" (Jonah 1:2, NRSV). God's heartfelt command couldn't be clearer, but Jonah is unwilling to go. So he squanders the nonviolent moment and tries to run away from God by getting on a ship to Tarshish.

But Jonah quickly learns that he cannot run away from God's presence. The sea becomes so troubled that the boat is in grave danger. Jonah eventually confesses to the crew that he has run away from God and now believes God is causing this raging storm because of him. So Jonah is hurled into the sea at his urging to spare the lives of others. The sea quiets down, and out of its depths a whale suddenly appears and swallows Jonah whole. Jonah spends three long days and nights in the whale's belly. From this damp and dark place he humbly prays for deliverance, and God extends a merciful hand by having the whale spew him onto dry land once again (see Jonah 1:4–2:10).

Having gotten Jonah's attention, God gives him a second chance. This time Jonah has the good sense to seize the nonviolent moment by doing as he is told. He goes to Nineveh, crying out, "Forty days more, and Nineveh shall be overthrown!" (Jonah 3:4, NRSV). His powerful words become the catalyst for conversion. The people listen attentively and are scared into action. They proclaim a fast, and "everyone, great and small puts on sackcloth" (Jonah 3:5, NRSV). The king decrees that "[a]ll shall turn from their evil ways and from the violence that is in their hands" (Jonah 3:8b, NRSV). As they turn away from evil, God turns toward them with mercy and spares Nineveh from the destruction that Jonah foretold.

In this story we see how far God will go to raise up reluctant prophets when society cries out for transformation. The Holy One was fed up with the injustices being done in Nineveh and was determined to do something to turn the situation around. When Jonah refuses to cry out as he's been told, God refuses to take no for an answer. God needs someone to awaken Nineveh to the evil in its hands and has decided that someone is Jonah. When Jonah finally makes his way to Nineveh to proclaim God's message, the people are moved to turn away from their wrongdoing. God is moved to withhold the city's destruction. And a city moves a little more toward justice and right relationship.

This amazing story has a lot to say about God's persistence in getting disciples to answer their call. When Jonah turns away from God, God goes after him. When Jonah is thrown into the sea, God sends a whale to give him safe harbor until he comes to his senses. And when Jonah beseeches God to save him, God tumbles Jonah out of the whale and into a new beginning. This holy persistence reminds us that each and every time we turn away from God, God turns toward us. The Holy One is always there to take us back and give us a fresh start. It reminds us, too, that when we squander a nonviolent moment for whatever reason, we can always change our mind and seize it.

We may find something of our own story in the example of Jonah as he runs away from God's call in his life. How many of us when faced with a similar call would run toward Nineveh rather than away? Jonah gives us permission to be honest with the fears that arise as we walk the way of discipleship. God knows our fears and our failings. God knows how to find us when we try to run and hide. God knows how to calm our fears and bolster our faith when we sit in darkness, like Jonah, longing for insight and understanding. And God knows what can happen to society if we refuse to answer God's call.

God longs for conversion in the heart of society today just as God longed for it ages ago. And so there is a need for disciples willing to answer the call to cry out against the injustice that is before God and us day after day. The story of Nineveh renews our hope that society can heed the call to conversion and change its ways. It offers a powerful example of a people engaged in a communal act of repentance. Yet it's hard to imagine the inhabitants of any city in our nation today donning sackcloth and proclaiming a fast to repent for the evil in their hands! Which is why we, like God, must persist. Our world is in need of the deep, soul-searching conversion that turned the city of Nineveh around. And so we must cultivate this conversion in the Nineveh neighborhoods and nations of today.

Years ago, I learned of a prophetic public action that creatively called for this kind of conversion. A group of peacemakers in Washington, D.C.

joined together in a symbolic action on Flag Day. They gathered in a public place with a large flag. They filled buckets with soap and water. Then they proceeded to scrub the flag. This flag needed to be cleaned, they explained, because it was sullied with the sins of our nation. They spoke specifically of the violence that was in our collective hands and the injustices being done in our names. Their scrubbing was a profound and prophetic way of calling attention to the social sins of our nation. Each person hard at work scrubbing that flag longed for our nation to repent of its wrongdoings. And each person who witnessed this action saw a powerful public outcry for our nation to change its ways.

This action offers a powerful example of prophets crying out against injustice in the public square. Instead of turning our backs on the offenses that occur around us daily, we must turn toward them. We begin by naming the social injustice we see. Like Jonah crying out in Nineveh, we give voice to the social sins in our midst and shed light upon the destruction these injustices cause. We give voice as well to our deep desire to repent of the violence in our hands and collectively change our ways. And we strive for the conversion of these injustices by giving ourselves to the way of nonviolence.

Even as we cry out against injustice in public, it's important that we also do so in private. As people of faith, we must bring to prayer the social injustices which burden our hearts and assault our souls. We lift up the sins of society and the people and places hurt by these sins. We lift up those who are in some way responsible for the wrongdoing as we beseech God's forgiveness. We ask forgiveness for ourselves as well when we are complicit with social sin. This rhythm of repentance assures that someone is acknowledging the world's transgressions and seeking God's forgiveness. Someone is praying that we, as a nation, repent of our wrongdoing and be cleansed of the violence in our hands. And someone is cultivating a rhythm of repentance in a world where it is deeply needed and desperately lacking.

This rhythm of conversion and repentance in our lives will lead us to new frontiers, much like Jonah's mission led him well beyond his comfort zone and John the Baptist's ministry led him far from the ways of the world. We may not find ourselves called to be desert dwellers like John, living apart from society in a barren land. We may not find ourselves cast by God into an unknown city to cry out against it. But the spirituality of nonviolence calls us into the wilderness nonetheless. Deep into the unknown it leads us, into the wilderness of our hearts and the untamed places of our souls. It calls us beyond a society where violence has become commonplace into the wilderness of another way. It calls us toward the wilderness of a heart covenanted to God's peace beating amidst a society covenanted to principalities and powers.

We enter into this wilderness anytime we face the misunderstanding of others that so often accompanies peacemaking. We come to know this wilderness when we advocate reconciliation in a society bent on retaliation. We experience it when we strive to live simply amidst a culture of overconsumption. The terrain can be rugged and relentless, and the challenges encountered can be legion. Yet the more our countercultural lives contrast with the conventional ways of society, the deeper into the wilderness we go.

Perhaps you can identify with a wilderness struggle I often experience. I am an American, living in a nation that prides itself on individualism and strength. I am also a Christian, a member of a faith tradition that values humility, care of community, and concern for the common good. I am a citizen of a nation that considers itself the world's greatest superpower. I am also among those deemed to be "citizens with the saints and also members of the household of God" (Eph 2:19, NRSV).

Living as a citizen of my homeland and of God's household can be a difficult thing to do. I live in the 20 percent of the world that consumes 80 percent of the world's resources. Yet my faith calls me to live in solidarity with those who are poor. My country is currently conducting military campaigns in several countries. Yet my faith calls me to love my enemies and pray for those who persecute me. Our nation is cracking down on immigrants and rounding up people suspected of terrorist ties or activities. Yet my faith calls me to love my neighbor as myself. This tug-of-war between my identity as a Christian and my identity as an American goes on and on, stretching me in two very different directions.

When the conduct of our nation pulls us in one direction while the canon of our faith yanks us in another, we are plunged deep into the wilderness. This wilderness is created when the way of nonviolence calls us to go against the grain of society. In this wilderness, words may be flung at us like arrows by angry people who disagree with us. There may be times when resistance to our message is so strong that we fear for our safety. Our nonviolent beliefs may be challenged to the core by virulent opposition and we may be marginalized or maligned because of the ideals we embrace. We may even be labeled as fools, traitors, or unpatriotic embarrassments to our nation's image.

I remember a time when I witnessed a seasoned peacemaker forging his way through this wilderness. We were part of a group of peacemakers involved in a demonstration at the Intrepid Sea, Air, and Space Museum in New York City. This museum is housed in a naval aircraft carrier that was active in World War II and Vietnam. The Gulf War was in full swing, and an exhibit in support of the war was being shown. We were there to protest the glorification of war and cry out against the violence being inflicted upon the Iraqi people.

During our demonstration, one of my fellow peacemakers began reciting some of the facts associated with the war. He called to mind and heart the suffering of the Iraqi people. He noted the destruction being done to Iraq as a result of the invasion combined with years of deadly sanctions. As he read, a visitor to the museum became enraged. The visitor marched up and began yelling vociferously, within inches of the protester's face, for what seemed like a long time. Yet this seasoned peacemaker held his ground. He did not flinch. He did not retaliate against the man spewing anger at him. He remained centered and faithful to the nonviolent endeavor in which we were all engaged.

This encounter is a fitting symbol of the wilderness we face when we cry out against injustice. The person who spewed anger expressed the sentiments of mainstream society. He mounted a challenge to ideas expressing a nonviolent point of view. The words that the peacemaker spoke represented the language of nonviolence. And his actions communicated a spirit consistent with his message. He stood there, rooted in his beliefs, enduring the anger of this man and the bewildered faces of onlookers. He stood on the edge of transformation, countering this verbal assault with the look and language of love.

Many of us who have taken a stand for justice can likely relate to this experience. We know what it's like to feel the icy stare of society upon us. We've experienced the sometimes-vehement reaction of those who disagree with us. We've stood in the footsteps of prophets gone before us as we've proclaimed truth to power and denounced the injustices being done in our names. This wilderness can be harsh, yet it is precisely where we need to be.

I journeyed deeper into this wilderness during my years as the national coordinator of Pax Christi USA. There were times when Pax Christi would take a prophetic stance or engage in a bold action for peace. On any number of these occasions, I received stinging criticism from members of society who disagreed with us. We had ruffled the feathers of the status quo, and they didn't like it. Over the years, I came to understand that the stronger the opposition, the greater the indicator that we were exactly where we needed to be. Like John the Baptist and Jonah, we were forging deep into the wilderness, pioneering a path for peace and facing every challenge that came our way.

In time, we'll recognize that the wilderness aspect of our peacemaking isn't just something we experience around us; it's also something we experience within us. There is a spiritual wilderness that we discover as our peacemaking journey brings us to new places in our souls. We will experience struggles similar to peacemakers and prophets who have gone before us, like the struggle of John the Baptist, who was tormented by people threatened by his teachings. We may taste the temptation of Jesus in the desert where he was enticed by Satan to embrace the way of worldly authority and wealth. We may be tempted, like Jonah, to run away and hide. We may feel the pain of the prophet's heart, burning with a vision too fierce to be contained and too unconventional to be accepted.

This wilderness can be a tough and scary place to be. We are likely to stumble as we step into a life made rugged by risk and rocky by uncertainty. There will be moments when we may be fooled into thinking that God has abandoned us to fend for ourselves. We will be tested by forces that tempt us to turn away from nonviolence and accept the world as it is. Yet even as we stumble over this stubborn terrain, winds of something very different whisper. We are not meant to endure the wilds of this place alone. The gentle voice of a wilderness God calling our names can be heard.

In this wilderness we come to know the God who sojourns with wilderness wayfarers as they pioneer new pathways and frontiers. We are comforted by a God who was milk and honey soothing the soul of John the Baptist. We are fed by a God who was daily bread broken to nourish the life of Jesus. We are grounded in a God who scooped Jonah out of the depths of the sea and delivered him safely upon dry land. We are guided by a God who led the Israelites through their wilderness journey and brought them back each time they lost their way. We are strengthened by a God who upholds wilderness wayfarers through every moment of struggle, a God who cradles every footstep taken in pursuit of peace.

Here we draw near to a God who dwells at the frontier of transformation between the world as it is and the world as God desires it to be. We empathize with the heartache of a God who beholds a world of too much chaos and too little compassion. We are embraced by a God whose faithfulness to nonviolence led to being mocked, scourged, laughed at, crucified, and buried. We are strengthened by a God who vanquished violence once and for all by rising from the dead. And we are cherished by a God whose love for us and for the way of nonviolence is everlasting.

The book of Exodus assures us of God's ongoing presence as it draws to a close the narrative of the Israelite's long and arduous wilderness journey. "The cloud rested on the Tabernacle in the daytime," Scripture tells us, "and at night there was fire in the cloud so that the whole house of Israel could see. And so it remained for every stage of their journey" (Exod 40:38, TIB). The Holy One is with us through each moment of every day and in every step along the way. God pitches a tent and abides with us no matter where the wilderness may take us. For God knows the way of peace passes through the wilderness. And the further into the wilderness we go, the closer to the promised land we come.

Questions for Reflection and Conversation

1. In what ways does the spirituality of nonviolence call you to conversion? What do you turn away from? What do you turn toward?

2. What role does repentance play in your life? What would it mean for you to develop a regular rhythm of repentance in your life?

3. Imagine people in today's world flocking to John the Baptist. He says to them, "Bear fruit worthy of repentance" and they ask him what they are to do. How might John respond? What are the fruits of repentance needed in your life and in our world?

4. In what ways does nonviolence lead you into the wilderness? What have you experienced in the wilderness and what have you learned from it?

5. How do you experience God's presence in the wilderness?

8

Rooted in God, Ready to Go Forth

SEIZING THE NONVIOLENT MOMENTS is not an easy thing to do. It doesn't happen automatically in a society where violence is much too prevalent. But our ability to seize these moments is strengthened when we take the time to cultivate a regimen of prayer and spiritual reflection. Without prayer, we can certainly practice nonviolence. But we cannot bring to our peacemaking the spirit that roots us in God and readies us for the challenges we face. And we cannot approach peacemaking from the vantage point of vocation as our faith calls us to do.

Jesus gives his blessing to peacemaking when he says, "Blessed are the peacemakers, for they will be called children of God" (Matt 5:9, NRSV). The US Catholic bishops not only give their blessing to this vocation but speak of it as a moral mandate. "Our biblical heritage and our body of tradition make the vocation of peacemaking mandatory," wrote the bishops on the tenth anniversary of their peace pastoral, *The Challenge of Peace*. "Our peacemaking vocation is not a passing priority . . . but an essential part of our mission to proclaim the Gospel and renew the earth."[1]

The way we live out our vocation will differ from person to person. No two peacemaking vocations will look exactly the same. Some may be called to pursue peacemaking as their primary work. Others live their vocation by seizing opportunities for peacemaking within the context of their daily lives. However we live out our vocation, it's important that we recognize it as an essential part of our Christian faith. "To be a Christian is to be a

---

1. National Conference of Catholic Bishops, *The Harvest of Justice is Sown in Peace*, "Concluding Commitments."

peacemaker," the bishops continued, "and to pursue peace is to work for justice."[2]

Peacemaking looks a little different when we view it in the context of vocation. We see it not only as something we do but as a part of who we are. It moves from the sidelines of our lives to the center and becomes an integral part of us. When we reflect on our vocation in prayer, we discern its meaning in the context of our lives. We deepen our understanding of what it means to approach peacemaking as an essential part of the faith we embrace. And we come to recognize the importance of prayer in the vocation of peacemaking.

Jesus modeled the essential place of prayer in the vocation he embraced. Prayer permeated his life as he sought out quiet places and contemplative moments in the midst of his very demanding vocation. He fasted and prayed for forty days in the desert to spiritually prepare before beginning his public ministry. Prayer gave him what he needed to withstand Satan, who placed the temptations of power, wealth, and worldly authority before him (see Luke 4:1–15). Each time Satan tried to lure him to the dark side, Jesus turned to faith as his stronghold by reciting Scripture verses from memory. His days and nights of prayer and fasting gave him the spiritual strength he needed to withstand the wily ways of evil.

Jesus turns to Scripture again when he goes to the synagogue in Nazareth to announce his vocation to all gathered there. He proclaims the words of the prophet Isaiah, saying, "The Spirit of our God is upon me: because the Most High has anointed me to bring Good News to those who are poor. God has sent me to proclaim liberty to those held captive, recovery of sight to those who are blind, and release to those in prison—to proclaim the year of our God's favor" (Luke 4:18–19, TIB). These words flow from the spiritual strength Jesus garnered in the desert as he overcame evil. "Today, in your hearing, this scripture passage is fulfilled," he continues (Luke 4:21, TIB). Jesus owns his vocation and states his intention to do everything in his power to fulfill it.

Prayer made it possible for Jesus to embrace his peacemaking ministry and it holds the same promise for us. Prayer grounds us in God and helps us remain centered in our efforts for peace. Without it, we can become like noisy gongs and clanging cymbals. The peace we proclaim with our lips rings hollow when it does not flow from a place deep within. This can happen when we focus on working for peace beyond ourselves without

2. Ibid., "Concluding Commitments."

working for peace within ourselves. It can happen, too, when we give our-selves to peacemaking without taking time for prayer. We can easily lose our footing and our sense of being grounded in God. Without prayer the spirit of nonviolence within us withers. And our peacemaking vocation loses its vitality.

I remember one of my seminary professors who spoke about the importance of prayer in a life of service. She told us about a pattern that emerged in the lives of people in ministry whom she supervised over the years. Those who cultivated a regimen of prayer thrived in their work and were enlivened by it. Those who didn't make regular time for prayer burned out again and again.

The wisdom of this professor holds important truths for us in relation to peacemaking. When we try to live a life of nonviolence, we go against the grain of a too-violent world. This labor exacts a heavy toll and can leave us feeling depleted. Prayer offers us a way to do the inner work we need to sustain ourselves. It fortifies the feeble places within us to withstand the challenges we face. It provides a spiritual harbor to release anger, pain, and anything that gets in the way of our work for peace. The stubborn places in us become supple enough to be channels of God's grace. And we find the inner resolve we need to follow where the journey beckons us to go.

While the Gospels give us a sense that prayer permeated the life of Je-sus, they don't provide much detail about the substance of his prayer. There is one Gospel passage, however, that illumines the prayer of Jesus unlike any other. It's the experience of Jesus praying through a long night in the garden of Gethsemane before his arrest. This Gospel story contains impor-tant truths about the power of prayer and its place within the spirituality of nonviolence. It also illustrates what can happen when we turn our will over to God.

The scene in the garden of Gethsemane takes place just after the Last Supper. Scripture tells us that Jesus arrives there deeply troubled, and for good reason. He has eaten with his disciples for the last time. He knows that Judas has gone forth to betray him. As Jesus walks to the garden with his disciples, Peter claims that he will never deny him and the other disciples also vow their allegiance. But Jesus knows better than to trust what they say. He knows them well enough to doubt their ability to withstand the challenges that lie ahead.

After entering the garden, Jesus says to the disciples, "Stay here while I go over there and pray" (Matt 26:36, TIB). He takes with him Peter, James, and John and reveals to them the agony he is experiencing deep within. "My soul is deeply grieved, to the point of death. Please, stay here, and stay awake with me," he says (Matt 26:38, TIB). On this night of all nights, Jesus does not want to be alone.

Jesus withdraws a little further into the garden, and the turmoil within his soul becomes more evident. He throws himself on the ground and begins to pray fervently. "Abba, if it is possible, let this cup pass me by. But not what I want—what you want" (Matt 26:39, TIB). These words reflect the deep discord that is tearing Jesus apart. We behold him at a moment of profound vulnerability as he admits to God his heartfelt desire to avoid the pain and persecution he knows is drawing near. At the same time Jesus somehow finds the words to pray for God's desire to overshadow his own.

Jesus is experiencing the turbulence of a heart torn between human and holy aspirations. He offers up his very human desire that the cup of persecution somehow escape his lips. Yet he knows remaining faithful to his earthly mission might render this desire impossible. And so he prays just as intensely to act in accordance not with his desire but with God's. It is one of Scripture's most intimate moments, as Jesus places his conflicted heart into God's consoling hands and surrenders himself as never before.

We can all relate to the conflicted heart that Jesus reveals in this story. We know what it's like to feel torn between human and holy aspirations. This happens whenever we find ourselves wrestling with ourselves and with God as we try to figure out the "right" thing to do in a given situation. We feel this tug-of-war whenever our conscience nags us over something we've done or something we may be thinking about doing. Sometimes we have a strong sense of what God is asking of us but we refuse to answer God's call. And we experience this inner conflict whenever we find ourselves stubbornly holding on to our desires for what we want rather than opening up to God's desires for us.

At times our oh-so-human hearts recoil from the difficult choices we are called to make when we follow the way of nonviolence. We may be called to sacrifice our comfortable way of life and accept a simpler lifestyle that is more sustainable for the planet. We may be asked to challenge the status quo by speaking out or taking action on behalf of those who are oppressed. We may feel called to take steps that lead us out of our comfort zone in new and very different directions. We may wonder how the way of nonviolence can possibly fit with our well-ordered lives and future plans. The cup we are given to drink will differ according to the ways we are called to live out our vocation. Like Jesus, there will be times when we plead that the cup of sacrifice might pass us by.

After praying for some time, Jesus rises and goes to his disciples and finds them fast asleep. Jesus says to Peter, "Couldn't you stay awake with me for even an hour? Be on guard and pray that you may not undergo trial. The spirit is willing, but the body is weak" (Matt 26:40–41, TIB). In the hours when Jesus most needs his disciples to remain vigilant with him, they slumber. He alone is keeping vigil through the darkest night of his life. He alone is attuned to the forces of darkness closing in upon him. In the company of God alone he is readying himself to remain faithful to nonviolence as he drinks the cup placed before him.

Jesus repeats this rhythm of returning to prayer and rising to be with his disciples two more times. Each time he goes to the disciples, he finds them still asleep. Each time he returns to prayer, he prays to be able to drink the cup of suffering if it is God's desire. As one darkened hour slips into the next, Jesus plumbs the depths of fear and faith in the company of God's love. Prayer helps to calm his soul as his fear slowly succumbs to the faith that has prevailed throughout his life. When Jesus rises from prayer for the final time, he does so fortified to face his future. He awakens the still-sleeping disciples and says, "Get up! Let us be on our way! Look, my betrayer is here" (Matt 26:46, TIB).

The transformation that has taken place in Jesus throughout his night of prayer is truly extraordinary. The fire of faith has melted his fears. He has moved from being daunted by what was to come to being determined to face it with courage. The key to this transformation lies in his willingness to open up to God's power at work in him. Prayer softens his grip on what he wants and empowers him for what God wants. Jesus finds what he needs to turn his will and his life over to God. By opening himself up in this way, he reveals the power of prayer in helping us to let go and let God.

Jesus begins his prayer by throwing himself on the ground in a gesture of total abandonment. He places his anguished heart before God and prays with the utmost honesty and humility. He doesn't pretend to have it all together. He doesn't try to hide his fears or his deepening despair. Jesus admits his powerlessness and his desire to put down the cup of suffering. He also confesses his desire to hand over his will to God so that God's will may be done.

By praying in this way, Jesus lets go of anything that may be standing between him and his Abba God. Freeing himself from these barriers frees him for the fullness of God's grace at work in him. His heart opens wide and he receives into his soul all that God longs to give him at this difficult time. While his betrayer is mobilizing forces against him, Jesus is mounting a spiritual defense. He begins his prayer with fear and trembling but rises from it rooted in God and ready to face those who have come to arrest him.

What does it mean for us to come before God in prayer this way? It means we go to God not in hiddenness but in honesty. We give ourselves wholeheartedly to God, knowing that sometimes we are simply a mess. Like Jesus, we offer to God all our fears and insecurities. We offer, too, all our frustrations, doubts, and despair. We release into God's hands all the consternation that is brewing within us. And that may include a reluctance to let go at all. We have a tendency to hold on to what we know rather than giving ourselves to the unknown. Letting go means we must loosen our grip on having things our way so that we can open our hands to God's way. And many of us find this kind of letting go a very difficult thing to do.

I know this struggle all too well. It's hard to admit sometimes how reluctant I can be to let go of my will so that God's will can be done in me. I dig in my heels and put God to the test as I let the tug-of-war begin. At times like these it helps to remember that Jesus struggled to hand over his will as well. He understands the tug-of-war taking place within me. He knows how reluctant I am to let go. He knows, too, that when I turn to him in prayer, he has the space he needs to slowly soften my stubborn heart. He is there to help me loosen my grip so that I can gradually give myself to God's way.

Opening ourselves up to God in this way leads us to inner freedom. We let go of the things that are holding us bound and the floodgates of God's grace open wide. We give God our whole hearts, including those parts that may be frightened or reluctant, and we receive wholeheartedly from God in return. Like Jesus in the garden, we receive the spiritual strength we need to drink whatever the cup of life may hold for us. This may not happen right away. Jesus had to keep returning to prayer to find what he needed to face his future with faith. So we must keep returning to prayer as well, believing that little by little we will find what we need to give ourselves to God's way.

The Gethsemane prayer of Jesus illustrates the importance of prayer in the spirituality of nonviolence. The contrast between Jesus and his disciples throughout the night in the garden couldn't be more striking. Jesus stays awake all night and falls to his knees in prayer so that he can be spiritually strengthened for what lies ahead, while the disciples fall asleep. They don't pray to prepare themselves for what is to come. They are awakened just before Jesus is arrested, and they are totally unprepared for all that is about to unfold.

What might have happened, I wonder, had the disciples stayed awake with Jesus throughout the night? Certainly they would have seen the anguish he was experiencing. They also would have seen the transformation that took place in him as he prayed throughout the night. Maybe they would have learned a lesson about the power of prayer in times of trouble. Perhaps they would have prayed to strengthen themselves spiritually to face what was ahead. Maybe they would have found what they needed to stand with Jesus during his time of trial.

Of course none of this happened because the disciples didn't remain awake. They didn't prepare themselves spiritually for the arrest of Jesus or the accusations that were to come their way. When they were put to the test, they were overcome with fear and spiritually uprooted. They responded with cowardice rather than courage. They gave in to the forces of darkness and gave up the way of nonviolent discipleship.

The words that Jesus spoke to his disciples cry out to us today with renewed urgency. "Remain here, and stay awake with me." What might this heartfelt plea mean for us as we strive to live out our vocation of peacemaking? It means that our work does not end when better times give way to bitter times. We are called to be vigilant about peace even when the darkness of our times seems deep and foreboding. Staying awake means that we watch, we wait, we witness, and we pray. We watch so that we might be attuned to the forces of violence that gather strength in the darkness. We wait for God's spirit to do its work in us. We witness by living out our vocation of peacemaking. And we pray to ground ourselves in God and receive the spiritual strength we need to follow wherever God calls us to go.

I learned something about staying awake for peace years ago when I attended all-night peace vigils at my church. Twice a year, a group of us would gather together in our cavernous church to pray for peace throughout the night. Peacemaking activities of all kinds enlivened these nights, with each one offered in a spirit of prayer. We watched educational videos on topics of justice. We wrote letters to government officials advocating for social change. We studied writings on nonviolence and discussed them in small groups. We folded peace cranes as we prayed for people and places in need of peace. These vigils were humble attempts to illumine the night's darkness with the determined light of peace.

As one sacred hour passed into the next, I thought about how fitting it was to keep vigil for peace from dark until dawn. Praying through the night reminded us of the importance of prayer amidst the darkened times in which we live. We learned the power of being with others in prayer when facing the forces of darkness. When dawn finally came, we went forth with bleary eyes and weary bodies. But we went forth renewed in spirit by the grace given to our souls through the stillness of the night.

Over the years I've learned that prayer is as important to the soul as sleep is to the body. In the sanctuary of prayer our lament mingles with our longing. We offer God whatever hesitancy we may have, and God offers us heartfelt love. God melts every fear we bring with the fire of faith. The longer we linger in these flames, the more we grow in intimacy with God. We take shelter in a God who huddles with the holy innocents suffering the consequences of violence. We shed tears with a God who weeps at the very thought of people taking up arms against each other. We stand in solidarity with a God whose passion for justice never wanes or wavers. We abide with a God who can fathom no other preemptive strike but love.

Prayer is an important doorway to a deeper relationship with Jesus and to solidarity with his suffering. When we take time to prayerfully contemplate the struggles of Jesus, we draw nearer to him in the anguished moments of his life. We tremble with him as he pleads, "If it is possible, let this cup pass me by." We let go with him as he says, "Not my will, God, but yours." We remain at the foot of the cross with him as he cries out, "My God, my God, why have you abandoned me?" The more we enter into solidarity with Jesus, the more we come to recognize his presence in our sufferings as we walk the way of nonviolence.

I remember discovering this in a powerful way a few years ago when I was praying to forgive someone who had betrayed me. I imagined myself there with Jesus in the garden of Gethsemane. I asked him to show me what it was like to be betrayed by Judas and abandoned by those closest to him. And I invited Jesus into my own experience of betrayal. The more I prayed, the more tenderness I felt for Jesus in his betrayal. And the more tenderness I felt from Jesus in my own experience. In time, my pain and anger began to melt away, and I became able to forgive. I never would have asked to be betrayed the way I was. But the hidden grace in this experience was a doorway to deeper intimacy with Christ that has strengthened me for the journey.

When we pray in this way, we deepen the spiritual roots that ground us for our vocation of peacemaking. We deepen our union with God. We become more able to withstand the temptations that try to tug us away from our peacemaking vocation. We foster an ever-greater integration between being a nonviolent person in private and bearing nonviolent witness in public. We grow in our ability to reflect an attitude of peace that flows from deep within. And we come to understand that the work of cultivating a culture of peace in society begins by cultivating a climate of peace in our souls.

One of the most prayerful peacemakers I have come to know over the years is Sr. Eileen Storey, SC. Sr. Eileen, who has taken her place among the communion of saints, was a professor, a peacemaker with a love for the Holy Land, and a woman of deep prayer. I came to know her in her later years as a strong and gentle woman of great wisdom. Her prayerfulness was evident in her being and in the way she lived her life. And it was especially evident in the way she lived out her commitment to nonviolence.

Sr. Eileen was a regular at public gatherings for peace in New York City. Oftentimes, we would both find ourselves at a demonstration or peace vigil which brought together all kinds of peacemakers. There were often a number of speakers representing many peace organizations. Some of these organizations were faith-based while others were not. Some of the words spoken advocated nonviolence while others did not. Too often, it seemed, words were spoken that were contrary to my own understanding of the spirit of nonviolence. Words of disrespect and derision, name-calling and negativity assaulted my ears. This type of message seemed to me to be destructive rather than constructive and made me uncomfortable. I wondered how I could authentically be a peaceful presence in the midst of such a demonstration.

At times like these, I turned my eyes toward Sr. Eileen. There she stood, staunch in her nonviolence. If words were being recited that she found offensive, she remained silent. But she expressed her discontent in her own strong yet gentle way. She stood there shaking her head with determination and offering her own silent prayer. She wagged her finger back and forth, letting it be known that she disagreed with the spirit of what was being said. She refused to leave because she believed in the cause of peace and wanted to be present. So she stayed, and her prayerful presence had a power that reached far beyond the shameful shouting that she quietly denounced.

Many years later, I remember this image of Sr. Eileen because it taught me an important lesson about the power of prayer and its place in the work of peace. Sr. Eileen's ability to be a prayerful presence was the fruit of her regular rhythm of prayer. Prayer permeated her life, and she was able to bring a prayerful presence to most everything she did, especially her work for peace. Prayer made it possible for her to be true to herself and her vocation. Her humble stance and quiet ways reminded me of the tender love of nonviolence. Her wagging finger reminded me of the tenacious love of nonviolence. She was to me an icon of holy resilience, a prophet of peace whose strength flowed from the heart of prayer. And through her prayerful presence nonviolence flowed into the heart of our world.

Prayer connects the peaceful work of our hands with the peaceful purposes of God's heart. We bring the transcendent presence of God into our transformative work for peace. This spirit of prayer unites us with one another in a bond that is deep and holy. We become part of something bigger than any one of us. And we bear witness to the reality that peacemaking is not something we take lightly. It is our vocation, and we approach it as an integral part of our Christian identity and an essential part of our discipleship.

Prayer joins us in spiritual communion with other peacemakers, past and present. We draw near to the martyrs who worked valiantly for peace and suffered unto death for their vigilance. We join with thousands of nonviolent disciples who have gone before us, all holy women and men who practiced nonviolence and left footprints for us to follow. We join in spirit with countless others who are committed to a life of prayer. Standing in the presence of this holy host, we are part of a great throng of pilgrims journeying through the long, dark night in search of a brighter tomorrow.

Our communion with this cloud of witnesses reminds us that the work of nonviolent transformation transcends time and place. We are involved in a spiritual endeavor that will continue long after our brief time upon this planet. Our nonviolent witness deepens the spiritual wells from which others will draw some day, as Sr. Eileen's deepened mine. And our work strengthens the spirituality of nonviolence passed from one generation of peacemakers to the next.

When I think of the spiritual strength we cultivate with God and others through prayer, I think of the image of the mighty sequoia tree. One might think that the roots of this giant tree reach deep into the ground to anchor it. But in reality the roots of this tree are relatively shallow. It is said that this tree gathers the strength it needs to soar high above other trees by stretching its roots far and wide. Sometimes the roots spread out to encompass an entire acre. Along the way, the roots of one sequoia find the roots of another. These roots wrap around each other, connecting one tree to the next. And the next. And the next, until the entire forest of sequoias joins together in an interwoven system of support buried beneath the surface. When strong winds blow and storms seek to topple them, it is the strength of these interconnected roots that holds the trees upright.

Through prayer, our spiritual roots become like the roots of the great sequoia tree. We root ourselves in the holy ground of God. We wrap our roots around those of others, anchoring ourselves in spiritual communion. We create a tapestry of support that weaves us deep into the fabric of God and one another. When clouds heavy with the thunder of a too-violent world loose their storms upon us, our roots hold us steady. When winds of adversity whip up and blow with all their might, our roots hold us firm.

Rooted in God and strengthened by the bonds we share with others, we come to know the power that flows from prayer. It is the power that enabled Jesus to get up from the Gethsemane ground where he knelt in confusion to go forth in courage. It is the power that readies us to withstand every tempest that troubles the nonviolent way. It is the power that endows us with the spiritual strength we need to live our vocation ever faithful to God's vision of peace.

Questions for Reflection and Conversation

1. Do you believe prayer is an important part of the spirituality of nonviolence? Why/why not?

2. How do you understand the term "vocation of peacemaking"? Do you consider peacemaking to be an essential part of the Christian faith? Why/why not?

3. What place does prayer hold in your life? How does it relate to your work for peace?

4. How have you experienced the struggle between holding tightly to your will or your way and handing your will over to God?

5. Have you ever been torn between wanting to work for peace yet being uncertain about enduring the struggle or sacrifice involved? How did you move beyond this impasse?

6. Do you try to cultivate peace within yourself while working for peace within society? How do these two forms of peacemaking relate to each other?

9

The Strength of Nonviolence in the Shadow of the Cross

A POWERFUL SYMBOL AROSE from Ground Zero in the days following the September 11 tragedies. Two days after the attacks, workers at the site came across the remains of two steel crossbeams that had been part of Tower One. These crossbeams somehow held together at their center when the building collapsed, and they emerged from the rubble in the shape of a cross. This cross quickly became a symbol of life and hope, and it was erected in a prominent place at Ground Zero. Its vertical beam reached upward toward the heavens as if beseeching God to enter this place of unspeakable horror. Its horizontal beam stretched outward like open arms longing for an embrace of tender mercy.

Each time I gazed upon this cross, I felt a strong connection to those whose lives are broken by violence. This cross stood strong for all whose lives were broken at Ground Zero and at other sites on September 11. It connected me to people around the world terrorized by brutal attacks and all those whose sense of security is blown to bits. I thought about the meager lives of those who dwell in poverty as I stood before the mountainous remains of buildings that were once soaring icons of prosperity. The cross rising from the ruins reminded me just how powerful a weapon hatred can be. In its shadow I pondered the relationship between the shattered remains at Ground Zero and the shattered lives of people impacted by heavy-handed US foreign policy.

In time I came to think of this cross as a powerful symbol of convergence. Terrorism had found its way into our nation, connecting us with people and places terrorized by violence around the world. This cross also symbolized a convergence between the orchestrators of violence and their victims. In this place where terrorists perished along with their victims, there was no denying that both victims and perpetrators of violence are connected by the brokenness that results. Here those who caused the violence were joined in death with those who suffered its consequences.

As I gazed upon this cross and pondered its symbolism for our nation, I thought about my own understanding of the cross. During my seminary years I was introduced to all kinds of theories about what the cross represented when Jesus was crucified and what it means in these times. There were those who thought of the cross as a horrible symbol of violence that represented the most excruciating form of execution. There were students from other countries who proudly wore the cross as a sign of strength, liberation, and hope. I wrestled with these ideas and theories as I grappled with my own understanding of this symbol that had become so important to me.

Over time, I came to embrace the cross as the place where violence, nonviolence, and faith come together in a spirit of transformation. Violence crucified Jesus on the cross and subjected him to an excruciating death. Nonviolence countered every violent action Jesus faced with the presence of love. And faith was the stronghold that supported him every step of the way, sowing seeds of transformation through it all.

The nonviolent moment that ultimately led to the crucifixion came as Jesus was being arrested on the Mount of Olives. It is perhaps the most pivotal nonviolent moment he ever faced, and it is captured in each of the Gospels. The account in Luke's gospel stands out because it most amplifies the message of nonviolence that flows from Jesus' actions.

In order to understand this moment in its fullness we must step back to a conversation that takes place at the Last Supper. Jesus has just shared a final meal with his disciples, and he is speaking to them one last time before going to the Mount of Olives. He reminds them that he once sent them out without a purse, a bag, or sandals and then suggests that things are about to radically change. "Now, however, the one who has a purse had better carry it; the same with a travelling bag," he says. "And if they don't have a sword, they should sell their cloaks and buy one! For I tell you what was written in scripture must be fulfilled in me: 'The suffering servant was counted among criminals'—for whatever refers to me must be fulfilled" (Luke 22:36–37,

TIB). The disciples then tell Jesus that they have two swords. Jesus replies, "That is enough" (Luke 22:38, TIB).

Imagine what it must have been like for the disciples to hear Jesus speaking like this! Suddenly their leader, whose ways were all about unconditional love and nonviolence, seems to be suggesting they take up arms. Finally, it seems, Jesus is willing to fight his adversaries with weapons rather than words. At long last his disciples will get the chance to defend him.

What might have been going through the mind and heart of Jesus as he spoke to the disciples in this way? Did he seriously consider offering armed resistance to those about to do him harm? Or was something else entirely happening?

After this conversation, Jesus enters the garden of Gethsemane and spends the night deep in prayer to ready himself for what lies ahead. We know from the previous chapter that Jesus wrestles in prayer to discern God's will for him. He comes to believe that he is called to drink the cup of suffering, and he finds the inner strength he needs to accept this call. Jesus recognizes that he has a choice in how he will face the events that are about to unfold. Will he retreat from nonviolence at this critical moment in order to defend himself and his legacy? Or will he find a way to extend the hand of nonviolence even as he is delivered into the arms of death?

Jesus emerges from his night of prayer, gathers his disciples, and is speaking with them as a crowd approaches. Judas comes forth from the crowd and betrays Jesus with a kiss to identify him as the one to be arrested. The disciples are eager to defend Jesus, and they have the weapons he told them to bring. "Rabbi, should we strike them with our swords?" asks one of the disciples, expecting Jesus to say yes (Luke 22:49, TIB). Before Jesus has time to answer the ear of the high priest's slave is cut off. Jesus quickly cries out, saying, "Stop! No more of this!" He confuses his disciples and thwarts their hopes of mounting an armed defense (Luke 22:51, TIB). He then reaches out to touch the slave's ear and tenderly heal it from the violence at hand.

In this poignant nonviolent moment there is a powerful convergence between violence and nonviolence. Those who came to take Jesus away are armed with swords and clubs. They are prepared to take Jesus by force if he doesn't go willingly. The disciples are ready to use their swords to defend Jesus, and one of them has already struck. Yet at a very volatile moment that could have easily erupted into battle, Jesus stands up unequivocally for nonviolence. He seizes the nonviolent moment with clarity and conviction.

He then affirms his choice by making his final act as a free person one of nonviolence. He extends an open hand of compassion as he tenderly touches and heals the ear of the injured slave. Jesus reaches across the battle lines drawn in the sand to touch one standing on the other side with a heartfelt gesture of peace.

How are we to understand this nonviolent action of Jesus after he told the disciples to arm themselves with swords? It's possible that Jesus intended to wage an armed battle the night before, but then thought differently after spending the night in prayer. It's possible that at the last moment he simply couldn't abandon his nonviolent ways in order to go through with his plan. But I believe Jesus never intended to have his disciples use the swords to strike. He told them to bring swords in order to fulfill the edicts of Scripture (see Isa 53:12). In the process, he realized he could teach them one great and final lesson about his unwavering commitment to the way of nonviolence.

The text gives us a clue that his intentions were nonviolent all along. When the disciples tell Jesus they have two swords, he tells them, "That is enough." Two swords are not nearly enough to defend him from the chief priests, temple police, and elders who came armed with clubs and swords to arrest him (see Luke 22:52). But two swords are more than enough to teach his disciples that they are to choose the way of nonviolence even when armed for battle.

There is a sense of urgency when Jesus tells his disciples to put down their swords, and for good reason. He was trying to prevent a bloodbath from taking place. Yet these words contain an important message that reaches beyond the moment at hand. Jesus is taking a final, powerful stand for nonviolence. "No more of this!" he proclaims, proving that he will not renounce the way of nonviolence even when it might be easy to choose the way of warfare. "No more of this!" he commands, urging his disciples to forsake violence once and for all. They are to renounce violence when they enter into a situation unarmed. And they are to renounce it even when they are gripping their swords tightly, ready to strike.

These words of Jesus came to mind as I reflected upon the cross at Ground Zero. "No more of this!" the cross seemed to cry out as it towered above the brokenness below. No more of the violence that leads to this kind of devastation. No more of the hatred that underlies such unspeakable acts of horror. And no more using our brokenness as an excuse to break others.

After his arrest, Jesus demonstrated just how serious he was about his desire to put an end to violence once and for all. His way of saying "No more of this!" was to journey to his death faithful to the nonviolence that formed the cornerstone of his life. He faced the haughtiness of his tormenters with humility and boldness of heart. Jesus endured being spit upon and scourged with the strength of his spirit. He persevered through unparalleled pain, refusing to retaliate in any way. There is nothing in the Gospels that suggests Jesus displayed even an iota of unkindness toward anyone who assaulted him during his passion. He stood up to every indignity thrust upon him with as much integrity as he could muster. Each time Jesus stumbled, he got up and pressed onward, displaying the strength of nonviolence to persevere in the face of the ultimate challenge.

Jesus remained faithful to nonviolence even when it appeared his life would end in defeat. He had been abandoned by his disciples and his nonviolent way was being vanquished by violence. Yet the Gospels illumine not the defeat of nonviolence during the way of the cross but its determination. Nonviolence remains faithful to its purpose even when it faces apparent failure. Why? Because it understands that what seems like a disappointing ending today will look like faithful endurance tomorrow. Each and every time it stumbles or falls, nonviolence gets up and continues onward. It does so recognizing that to continue onward is not an exercise in futility. It's an example of faithfulness.

Nonviolence looks upon its endeavors by taking the long view. We cannot know where the nonviolent steps we take today may lead tomorrow. We must hold fast to the wisdom of Gandhi, who said that nonviolence is an experiment in truth. When it comes to nonviolence, we are constantly experimenting. Some of our experiments will succeed. Others may fail. The important thing is that we keep trying. For each time we experiment by seizing the nonviolent moment, the power of nonviolence grows stronger.

This is important to remember when we find ourselves standing before the cross. We all know what it's like to face the crosses of our lives, those times when we feel hurt or even crushed by someone or something. We know what it's like to endure suffering, hardship, or struggle. We can identify with the suffering of Jesus at times when we feel belittled, betrayed, beaten down, or hung out to dry.

When we find ourselves facing the cross, we face a particularly challenging nonviolent moment. How can we believe in the power of nonviolence when we are feeling beaten down, crushed, or crucified? The pain of the cross can be so intense that we might question or even abandon our nonviolent beliefs. We're much more likely to think about relief from our pain or even retaliation toward those deemed to be responsible. Indeed, nonviolence may be the furthest thing from our minds when the weight of the cross presses down upon us.

When the forces against us cause our resolve to waiver, it is the image of Jesus, beaten down yet forging ahead faithful to nonviolence, that inspires us to persevere. The resiliency of this nonviolent spirit is captured by Paul in his Second Letter to the Corinthians. "We are afflicted in every way possible," he writes, "but we are not crushed; we are full of doubts, but we never despair. We are persecuted, but never abandoned; we are struck down, but never destroyed. Continually we carry about in our bodies the death of Jesus, so that in our bodies the life of Jesus may also be revealed." (2 Cor 4:8–10, TIB).

No matter how hard it may seem, Paul says, we are never to give into despair or allow ourselves to be destroyed by the forces at work against us. This may be easier said than done. Yet the more we ground ourselves in the spirituality of nonviolence, the more we come to know its resiliency and constant hope. If we give into despair or allow ourselves to become constrained, we sacrifice our power at the hands of whatever is afflicting us. So we choose instead to draw our power from the Nonviolent One whose strength withstood the ultimate persecution.

When we walk the way of nonviolence we come to know the affliction that Paul knew. We are afflicted by the violence that assaults our world and feel as if our efforts for peace are in vain. We know, too, what it is to be perplexed. We live in perplexing times that make it difficult to know what is needed to bring about genuine and lasting peace. And many of us know what it's like to be put down or persecuted because of our nonviolent beliefs.

In the midst of all of this, we are not to allow ourselves to be destroyed or driven to despair. We may not know the way of the future, but we know the way of nonviolence. Like Jesus as he walked to Calvary, we pave the pathway of the future by giving ourselves nonviolently to the present. When we fall, we dig deep to find the spiritual strength to get up. We walk in the spirited footsteps of Jesus, who journeyed in faith despite the weight of the world pressing down upon him. He would not let the way of nonviolence be dismantled by those seeking to destroy him, no matter how hard they tried. He got up and gave every ounce of his strength to the way of the cross, empowering the way of nonviolence through his witness.

Carrying the dying of Jesus within us means that we carry in our hearts the way of nonviolence. We carry the words he spoke as he was being arrested, making his "no more of this" a type of mantra we recall in our nonviolent living. We remember these words when we are tempted to give up or give into the culture of violence. We recall them when we are on the verge of retaliating in word or deed for some wrong done to us. And we remember them when we become aware of something that is unjust and know deep within that we need to act. These words call us to break the cycle of violence again and again by giving ourselves to the way of nonviolence.

When we carry within us the dying and rising of Jesus in this way, we deepen our solidarity with the body of Christ being crucified in our world today. And we deepen our solidarity with the spirituality of nonviolence. We tap into the wellspring of nonviolent power that brings strength to our weakness and anchors us for the nonviolent way that we walk.

This nonviolent power is boldly and beautifully proclaimed through the life of Rigoberta Menchú, a Nobel Peace Prize laureate who has devoted her life to fighting for justice, human rights, and the dignity of indigenous peoples. Born into an impoverished Quiché family in Guatemala, Rigoberta became active in social reform activities through the Catholic Church when she was a teenager. Both of her parents and her brother were killed during the long years of war and oppression of her people. Yet she remained active in groups who were standing up for the human rights of the oppressed. She joined those who were educating and organizing the indigenous people to offer nonviolent resistance to massive military repression by the government. Eventually, she went into hiding, fled her country, and has worked from abroad for the liberation of her homeland and the rights of indigenous peoples throughout the world.

Rigoberta knows what it means to carry the dying of Jesus within her. In her autobiography, she shares words spoken by her sister that remain in her heart. "A revolutionary isn't born out of something good," her sister said. "He is born out of wretchedness and bitterness. . . . We have to fight without measuring our suffering, or what we experience, or thinking about the monstrous things we must bear in life."[1]

The strength of these words capture the strength of Jesus as he walked the way of the cross. He did not let the monstrous weight of what he was

---

1. Menchú, *I, Rigoberta Menchú*, 237.

bearing defeat him. He carried on without measuring his suffering or counting the cost. Jesus reached deep within himself to find the faith needed to endure. He stood strong in his nonviolence, and he calls us to do the same.

When Jesus commands his followers to forsake violence as he is being arrested, he does not leave them defenseless. He does not tell them to give up or give in to their adversaries even when it seems that things are falling apart. Jesus tells them to put down the weapons of warfare that will only bring about harm. He invites them to put on the armor of nonviolence instead.

This armor is beautifully described in a Scripture passage from Paul's Letter to the Ephesians. Paul calls his disciples to stand firm before the principalities and powers of their time. "[D]raw your strength from Christ and from the strength of that mighty power" writes Paul (Eph 6:10, TIB). "You must put on the armor of God if you are to resist on the evil day and, having done everything you can, to hold your ground. Stand fast then, with truth as the belt around your waist, justice as your breastplate, and zeal to spread the Good News of peace as your footgear. In all circumstances, hold faith up before you as your shield; it will help you extinguish the fiery darts of the Evil One. Put on the helmet of salvation, and carry the sword of the Spirit, which is the word of God" (Eph 6:13–17, TIB).

This is the armor that strengthened Jesus to persevere through the persecution he faced in life and in the shadow of death. It protected Paul and the early Christians as they withstood the principalities and powers of their day. And it is the armor that shields Christians walking the way of nonviolence today, giving us all the mettle we need. Clothed in this way we can never be entirely stripped of our power or our dignity even in the face of the staunchest opposition. We have what we need to stand firm in our faith. We have what we need to stand strong in the truth of nonviolence. "Faith and strength go together," says Pope Francis as he speaks about the power of Christian love. "The Christian is not violent, but he is strong. And with what strength? That of meekness, the force of meekness, the force of love."[2]

Whenever we face the crosses of our lives, the invitation is not to give up. It is to stand strong in the power of love that is at the heart of our Christian faith. We stand strong in the face of the cross because it is what nonviolence requires of us. And we stand strong because we never know what lies beyond the moment at hand. We must remember that the cross

2. Pope Francis, "Address to the Faithful Gathered in St. Peter's Square."

is the place where the sting of violence meets the strength of nonviolence. And when we bring the power of nonviolence to bear upon the crosses of our lives, we open up the possibility of transformation.

What would have happened to the segregated South if marchers in the civil rights movement had given up each time they were hosed down, beaten by police, or bitten by guard dogs? What would have happened in Poland if the young Solidarity movement that eventually ushered in democracy had given up after initially being repressed by martial law? And what would have happened to the future of India and its nonviolent movement, birthed by Gandhi and the salt marchers, if those who dared to resist the repressive British rule had given up when beaten by guards as they entered the salt mines? Each of these nonviolent movements eventually achieved its desired goal. And all of them made important contributions to the growth and development of nonviolence in the process.

Whenever a person or community faces violence with the strength of nonviolence, transformation takes place in some way or another. This transformation may be soft or subtle. It may be deep and lasting. Or it may be something happening at a level far beyond our ability to see. Maybe we are the ones being transformed through our nonviolent witness. Maybe those who are caught up in the violence with us are being transformed. Or maybe the seeds of transformation are being planted to sprout and grow at a later time.

A prophetic example of this transformation is evident in a group of people profoundly impacted by the soul-shattering violence of September 11. Each member of this group lost a loved one in the attacks. All of them suffered unfathomable anguish as a result. They were brought face to face with violence that was beyond anything they could ever have imagined. Yet each of them realized in the depths of their agony that they did not want others to suffer as a result of their loss. Deep down, beneath all of the anguish and heartache, something was stirring, and they were able to respond from that place. They faced a nonviolent moment unlike any before. And in the midst of their suffering they seized it.

Somehow these extraordinary people found each other and formed an organization known as September 11th Families for Peaceful Tomorrows. Members of this group choose to remember their lost loved ones in a spirit of reconciliation rather than retaliation. Over the years, they have mingled their tears with those of families who have lost loved ones in Afghanistan and Iraq. They have held in their arms the mother of Zacharias Moussaoui, the alleged twentieth hijacker in the September 11 attacks, and spoken words of mercy to her. They have organized an exchange of letters between US and Iraqi students to build bridges of understanding amidst the brokenness of war. They reach out with heartfelt understanding to those who have lost loved ones in other terrorist attacks and stand in solidarity with victims of violence around the world. In all that they do, they are transforming their grief into a groundswell for peace.

The nonviolent witness of September 11th Families for Peaceful Tomorrows is worthy of worldwide attention. They have been ridiculed and rejected by those who deem their actions to be unpatriotic. Yet these brave souls have remained firm in their nonviolent convictions in the face of persecution. Their witness proclaims that it is possible to sow seeds of new life amid the ashes of death. They are revealing the power of compassion to conquer hatred. They are proving that broken hearts find their way toward healing not through revenge but through reconciliation. And they are showing our world that it can move beyond its fear of global terror to work for global transformation.

Colleen Kelly, one of the cofounders of September 11th Families for Peaceful Tomorrows, lost her brother Bill at the World Trade Center. She herself is a Christian who echoes the sentiments of Pope Francis about the love we are called to put into practice. Shortly before the tenth anniversary of September 11, she listened to a rabbi who spoke at a conference she attended. In the months following the attacks, Rabbi Irwin Kula began seeking out the last words of those who died on that tragic day.

> "And you know what he discovered?" writes Colleen. "Not a single person said 'Kill them' or 'Avenge my death.' . . . Ultimately, and overwhelmingly, the last words of those killed on 9/11 were about love. 'Tell mom and dad I love them.' 'Tell the kids I'll miss them and I love them.' 'Julie, it's bad, but know that I love you.'"[3]
>
> "So what do these last words tell us?" Colleen continues. "I like to think they teach a lesson. There's a time for righteous moral outrage, just as there's a time for accountability, and justice. . . . But in the end, it's about love . . . [a]nd how much I want the world to be a place where last words are never the end result of political violence, but instead reflect a full and just life, well lived."[4]

3. Pax Christi USA, *Peaceweavings*.

4. Ibid.

SEIZING THE NONVIOLENT MOMENTS

I ponder these prophetic words alongside the powerful symbol of the cross at Ground Zero. I call to mind the many crosses of our world, and the arresting words of Jesus fill my heart. "No more of this!" groans Ground Zero, which once cradled brokenness beyond belief. "No more of this!" proclaim the members of September 11th Families for Peaceful Tomorrows as they stand strong against vengeance and violence. "No more of this!" shouts a world weary with the weight of too much violence. "No more of this!" pleads the universal body of Christ, begging for release from its suffering.

These cries are being heard and amplified by Christian leaders who are echoing the urgent plea of Jesus. "We must join with Pope John Paul II," wrote the US Catholic bishops in their pastoral message, "to 'proclaim, with all the conviction of my faith in Christ . . . that violence is unacceptable as a solution to problems, that violence is unworthy . . . Violence is a lie, for it goes against the truth of our faith, the truth of our humanity.'"[5]

Our faith calls us to proclaim "No more of this!" to the violence that poisons our hearts and crucifies our society. No more pretending that violence can resolve the problems that plague our world. No more ignoring the reality that violence begets violence. No more accepting the lies of war-waging governments while ignoring the cries of the war's victims. No more acting as if the inhumanity of violence is a humane way to resolve our differences. And no more believing that violence can be redemptive. The way of redemption is the way of the cross. And the way of the cross is the way of nonviolence.

I dare to hope that one day our nation will understand that we cannot use violence to root out violence. Perhaps one day we will realize that the violence we impose on others will eventually find its way back to us. Maybe some day we can admit that there needs to be a radical shift deep within the soul of our nation. A shift away from domination to diplomacy. A shift away from combat to collaboration.

Jesus taught us that violence must be met again and again with nonviolence. That is the message of the cross, the enduring symbol of our faith. The cross reminds us that Jesus chose nonviolence even in the face of death for the sake of a world transformed. We become part of this transformation whenever we counter the cruelty of violence with the courage of nonviolence. This is the transformation that long ago converted the cross from a place of bloodshed to a place of blessing. And it is this transformation that

5. US Conference of Catholic Bishops, *Confronting a Culture of Violence*, Section II, "A Culture of Violence."

can be the bridge between the pain of these troubled times and the promise of brighter tomorrows.

Questions for Reflection and Conversation

1. What does the cross symbolize for you? Have you ever thought about it as a place where violence comes together with nonviolence?

2. Do you believe nonviolence has the power to endure even when facing the cross? Why or why not?

3. Have you ever been tempted to give up on nonviolence in general or on a particular nonviolent effort? What has helped you to go on?

4. When your efforts at nonviolence lead you to apparent failure, what do you do?

5. In what ways do you say, "No more of this!" to violence? How is this evident in the way you live your life?

6. Imagine yourself putting on the "armor" of God as described in Scripture by Paul (see Eph 6:13–17). How do you outfit yourself spiritually to face the forces against you nonviolently?

10

Answering the Call to Rise

EMILY DICKINSON ONCE WROTE, "We'd never know how high we are, till we are called to rise; and then, if we are true to plan, our statures touch the sky."[1] I love this quote in general. And I especially love it when I think about it in the context of the spirituality of nonviolence.

Each time we face a nonviolent moment, we are asked to rise to the challenge before us. We may find ourselves wanting to respond in kind to someone who hurt us, all the while knowing we are called to rise above the urge to retaliate. We may be tempted to go along with others in society who advocate an eye for an eye rather than remembering that this kind of behavior makes the world blind. Or we may simply want to lay low and retreat from the call to rise rather than standing tall in our nonviolent truths. Yet when we are able to answer the call to rise, we grow in stature. And the stature of nonviolence grows as well.

Nonviolence is a resilient life-force with the power to lift society to a better way of being. It raises up a way of life defined by love in a culture of too little loving. It lifts the yoke of oppression from the backs of exploited people and moves them toward liberation. Nonviolence lifts communities beaten down by aggression and moves them toward right relationship. Violence, on the other hand, drags us down. It hardens our hearts and diminishes our dreams. It leads to division, hatred, and fear while causing chaos and confusion. Worst of all, violence deadens us as it draws us into a downward spiral of destruction.

---

1. Dickinson, *The Quote Garden*.

In his First Letter to the Corinthians, Paul writes, "We are fools for the sake of Christ. . . . When reviled, we bless; when persecuted, we endure; when slandered, we speak kindly" (1 Cor 4:10, 12b-13a, NRSV). Paul is calling his followers to rise above the opposition they face in the spirit of nonviolence. This is quite a summons, similar to the call of Jesus to love our enemies. It's hard to rise up from the pain of being slandered to speak kindly. It's even harder to rise up from being reviled to bless the one who reviled us. Sometimes it's all we can do to rise up just enough to keep from saying something unkind or doing something spiteful. How are we to find it within ourselves to speak kindly or even to bless?

Paul realized it's foolish in the eyes of the world to act like Christ. Yet he also recognized it's faithful and wise in the eyes of Christ. Paul understood that when we respond to violence with violence, we give destruction the final word. And so he calls us to rise up in the face of violence to give transformation the final word. When we meet hatred with kindness or injustice with mercy, we halt the destructive course of action, at least for a moment. We choose the high road, so to speak, rather than lowering ourselves to the level of violence. Acting this way goes against the grain of society and may be looked upon as utterly ridiculous. But in the eyes of God it is utterly right. In that moment, our statures stretch upward toward the skies. We rise up beyond the world as it is toward the peaceful world as we desire it to be.

There is one Gospel story that I find especially poignant as we consider how nonviolence is calling us to rise today. It is John's resurrection account of Mary Magdalene at the tomb of Jesus. At this tomb Mary answered the call to rise. And from this tomb Mary went forth as an agent of resurrection.

Mary arrives at the tomb with a heavy heart the morning after Jesus' death. She discovers that the stone has been removed and the body of Jesus is not there. Her heart sinks even further into despair. Thinking his body has been taken, she goes to fetch Peter and the disciple whom Jesus loved. When they see what has happened, they don't know what to make of it. The disciples have been led to believe empty promises and now must contend with an empty tomb! It is too much to bear. Bewildered and fearful, Peter and the other disciple depart from the tomb and return to their homes (see John 20:1–10).

But Mary remains. Suddenly, she hears a voice asking her, "Why are you weeping? For whom are you looking?" (John 20:15a, TIB). Mary turns to face the resurrected Jesus but does not recognize him. "Please, if you're the one who carried Jesus away," she implores, "tell me where you've laid the body and I will take it away" (John 20:15b, TIB). Jesus responds simply, saying, "Mary!" Mary's heart leaps as she recognizes the voice of Jesus, and she exclaims, "*Rabboni!*" meaning "Teacher" (John 20:16, TIB). Her eyes open to behold the risen Jesus and she begins to see that her world is forever changed.

Jesus tells Mary not to hold on to him since he has not yet made his ascent to God. She is to hold on to the reality of his resurrection instead. She must let the truth of all the astonishing things that are happening sink deeply into her soul. Jesus invites her to breathe in the power of this resurrection moment and let it resound throughout her being. He wants Mary to understand the meaning of his resurrection in her life and in the life of the other disciples. They must now take responsibility for continuing the nonviolent way that Jesus began. Like Jesus, the time has come for them to answer the call to rise.

Jesus sends Mary forth, saying, "go to the sisters and brothers and tell them, 'I'm ascending to my Abba and to your Abba, my God and your God!'" (John 20:17, TIB). What does Jesus want the disciples to hear in these words? He wants them to understand he is rising from the dead. And he wants them to believe all he has told them. It's as if he is saying, "All that I taught you is true. Everything I said would happen is happening. I am answering God's call to rise and so must you. Rise up, go forth, and continue the work I began."

Whatever may have gone through the mind and heart of Mary as she stood before the risen Jesus, she found what she needed to answer the call to rise. As she makes her way to the disciples, I imagine her pondering all that has happened and all that Jesus said would happen before he died. These things look radically different in the light of the resurrection. Mary now knows that the death of Jesus was not the end of his nonviolent way. There is much more to come, much more to be discovered, and much more rising to be done in his name.

Mary finds the other disciples and shares with them the news of his resurrection. She tells them what he has said to her and invites them to join with her in answering the call of the risen Christ. They who abandoned him must now confess and confirm their identity as his disciples. The time has come for them to rise up and continue forging the nonviolent way that Jesus so earnestly began.

In the rising of Jesus from death to new life, nonviolence rises as well. This extraordinary event is God's crowning nonviolent moment. The resurrection of Jesus is God's resounding "no" to violence and earthshaking "yes" to nonviolence. Raising Jesus from the dead raises up the way of life he lived. The unconditional love of Jesus that seemed to fail now conquers the grave. The way of nonviolence rises up victorious from its apparent defeat. The resurrection of Jesus becomes the catalyst for nonviolence to rise up to even greater heights through the lives of the disciples.

And that is exactly what happens. After failing Jesus in his final hours, his followers rise up. Given the power to teach, heal, and forgive, they travel near and far doing just that. They proclaim a God of unconditional love, a God who shows no partiality and transcends every border dividing the human family. They are imprisoned repeatedly for proclaiming and following the nonviolent way of Jesus. No matter what happens to the disciples, no matter how much persecution they endure, they rise up and continue onward. They do not waiver from the way of nonviolence even in the face of death. Instead they raise its stature as high as they possibly can.

I found myself pondering the Christian call to rise in the months following the September 11 tragedies. During these months I visited Ground Zero a number of times as the cleanup and recovery effort was underway. Each time I was there, the landscape of loss changed as more of the remnants and remains were removed. When the dedicated workers completed their mission, what remained was a gaping hole in the heart of our city and nation. I was overcome by the sheer emptiness of this vast open space where the towers had been each time I saw it. Those gleaming towers had reached high into the sky and had a huge presence. Now, this silent, cavernous space testified to the enormity of all that was lost.

As I prayed at the edges of this wide open space, I realized that Ground Zero had become an empty tomb. The broken bodies and sacred remains had been removed along with the remnants of shattered buildings. But the shadow of death remained.

I thought about Mary weeping before the empty tomb of Jesus as she realized her life was forever changed by all that it represented. I thought about how the life of our nation was forever changed by this tomb before me. War was quickly becoming a way of life. Fear of another terrorist attack had settled deeply into our nation's soul. This empty tomb brought home to me as never before the stark and sobering reality of what violence does to us as a people. It gouges life out of our world and sucks life from our souls. It leaves behind hollow remains where hallowed lives once thrived.

Each time violence breaks out in our world it creates a tomb of sorts. Whether a particular instance of violence is fatal or not, it inevitably leads to loss. Violence robs us of the sense of security we seek. It leads to broken lives, fractured relationships, and shattered dreams. It scars the soul of our society and it diminishes us as a people. "Violence is not the solution," wrote the US Catholic bishops in their pastoral message on violence. "[I]t is the most clear sign of our failures."[2]

At Ground Zero I thought about how Mary rose to the challenge given her by the risen Christ. I knew this tomb before me was nothing like the tomb of Jesus. Yet it was empty, like his. And like his, this tomb once cradled the bodies of those whose lives were taken at the hands of violence. What would it mean for Christians today to follow in the footsteps of Mary, I wondered. What would it mean to raise the stature of nonviolence in a deflated post-September 11 world? And what rising could possibly be born from so much dying?

I left the empty tomb pondering these weighty questions. Months later, something happened that helped me find the answers I was seeking.

Each year on September 11, family members of those who died at Ground Zero gather there for a remembrance ceremony. One anniversary fell on a beautiful, blustery day a year or two after the tragedy. The wind whipped up and blew strong as the ceremony got underway. All was going according to plan when suddenly the wind gusted with a great rush, stirring up a swirl of ash and dust from the depths of Ground Zero. This swirl of sediment rose high above the heads of all gathered as if carried by the breath of the spirit. It wafted heavenward in a beautiful, upward spiraling motion that resembled incense rising. It was as if the spirits of those whose lives ended there were visibly present, rising up on the breath of new life.

This image captivated me the moment I saw it. It felt like the spirit of resurrection that visited the empty tomb of Jesus had come to breathe resurrection upon this empty tomb. For one brief and breathtaking moment, the spirits of those who gathered here were lifted as their eyes turned heavenward. Because this image was captured by the media, its reach extended far beyond Ground Zero. All who saw it were touched by the transforming

---

2. US Conference of Catholic Bishops, *Confronting a Culture of Violence,* Section II, "A Culture of Violence."

power of the spirit as they joined together in silent solidarity at this empty tomb.

There was something sacred about the way the ashes rose that day. Their rising provided a sense of reassurance that those who perished there were at peace. I had the sense that these rising ashes were calling us to rise as well. It was as if the breath of resurrection had come to this empty tomb to breathe new life into us as a people. Find it in your hearts to rise above the lethal ways of war to pursue the long-lasting way of peace, this spirit seemed to say. Rise like a phoenix from the ashes of September 11 and go forth from this empty tomb as agents of resurrection.

This is the rising that was begging to be born from so much dying. But it was far from happening at that time. In the aftermath of September 11, our nation set out on the long, winding road of retaliation. We waged war on Afghanistan as a direct response to September 11. We invaded Iraq in 2003. Since then, we have been directly involved in military campaigns there and in Pakistan, Yemen, Somalia, Libya, and Syria. The road of retaliation has taken us far from the nation we used to be. Polls show that more Americans today hold an unfavorable view of Islam than in the months following the September 11 attacks.[3]

"Does anyone harbor anger against another and expect healing from the Lord?" writes the author of Sirach (Sir 28:3, NRSV). This Scripture text just happened to be the assigned Scripture for the tenth anniversary of September 11. As I prayed with it, I realized how we as a nation had harbored our anger for a full decade. We had hardened our hearts and dug in our heels because of the horrors done to us. Many would say we had good reason to do so. But is it any wonder that our spiritual and emotional wounds haven't healed?

I remember the celebrations that followed the killing of Osama Bin Laden in 2011. I was particularly struck by the prominence of young adults who seemed especially jubilant. A Jesuit priest at a nearby Catholic college made the point that Osama Bin Laden was like Hitler to this college generation. These students were young when the tragedy of September 11 happened, he explained, and they had been raised to believe that he was public enemy number one. They had been fed a steady diet of hatred toward him and other terrorists during their formative years. Should we be surprised to see them respond in this way?

3. Pew Forum Poll, "Only a Minority."

At this college, like many others, hundreds of students came together to rally in celebration. They waved American flags as they sang, "We are the champions of the world." At this same rally five courageous students conveyed a very different spirit by holding a sign which read, "Is this justice?" One of these students explained, "We wanted to address whether fighting violence with more violence is truly the right answer."[4] These five students faced significant taunting from the other students, and eventually their humble sign was snatched away. Still they remained, standing strong and vigilant, holding up their fingers in a sign of peace.

"When reviled, we bless," wrote St. Paul to his disciples. "When persecuted, we endure; when slandered, we speak kindly" (1 Cor 4:12b-13a, NRSV).

These students answered the call to rise. And they seemed to understand what so many in our world do not. Ours is a world where too many tombs are filled with the truncated remains of people killed in an unending cycle of violence. The longer we use violence to try to solve the problem of violence, the longer we will stand facing the darkened tombs we create, unable to see the light of another way.

Nonviolence invites us to turn away from our death-dealing ways so that we can begin to heal the hollow places born of September 11. This means we must turn away from violence toward a new way of being. We must answer the call to rise above our history of retaliation to engage ourselves in the work of reconciliation.

All of us must answer this call to rise in our own way. In their pastoral message on violence, the US bishops called for responding to violence and the threat of violence in society by bringing "new energy and creativity to the vocation of peacemaking."[5] This call, issued in a pre-September 11 world, is even more urgent today. New energy is needed to infuse our vocation with new voices and fresh vision. Creativity is needed to raise the stature of nonviolence to heights never before attained. This energy and creativity can be kindled in all of us with a little coaxing or inspiration. And it is easily kindled from tiny spark to blazing fire in the hearts of those who are young.

Let me share with you a story that illustrates what I'm trying to say. Years ago, I was involved in planning a national conference on peace and

4. Schaeffer-Duffy, "The Cross and the Sword," 1.

5. U.S. Conference of Catholic Bishops, *Confronting a Culture of Violence*, Section VI, "Conclusion."

justice. Those of us on the planning team wanted a dramatic visual to display throughout the weekend. We came up with the idea of placing a huge balance on stage, the kind with a pan on either side. One side of the balance represented the injustice of the world. The other side represented justice and peace. How powerful it would be, we thought, to have participants place stones on the side of justice throughout the conference. Each stone would represent their individual actions for peace. All of these stones together would present a powerful image of their collective actions. And this growing pile of stones would tip the scale slowly yet steadily toward justice.

The conference began with the balance heavily weighted on the side of injustice. It brought home in a stark way the weight of oppression hanging heavily upon our world. Near the justice side of the balance we placed a large container of stones. Conference participants were invited to ponder actions they had taken for peace. Each time they thought of one, they were to take a stone and place it on the side of justice. As they did, we invited them to think about these stones as symbols of the nonviolent power and potential that lies within each of us.

Stones were gradually placed on the balance as the conference went on. Each day, the scale moved ever so slightly. When the final morning of the conference arrived, those of us planning it grew concerned. The balance had shifted somewhat, but it still hung heavy with the weight of the world's injustice. We worried that the scale might not shift in favor of justice before the conference ended. If it failed, our dramatic symbol would be a flop, and people would leave the conference with a huge visual of injustice prevailing in our world!

The time came for our closing liturgy, and during the offertory procession people approached the scale one by one. The steady stream of people placing their stones symbolized the importance of the nonviolent choices we make each day. The growing pile of stones was a powerful image of the momentum we build when we join together in the nonviolent transformation of our world. Each stone moved the scale ever so slightly, yet with each stone the spirit of hope that filled the room grew stronger. You could feel the deep desire in the hearts of all gathered to right our unbalanced world and finally tip the scale in favor of justice.

After many people had placed their stones and returned to their seats, a young man approached the scale with his toddler daughter. Like those before him, he placed his stone on the side of justice. He helped his daughter place her stone on the pan as well. And then he did something entirely unexpected. He lifted his daughter up high and with great fanfare placed her on the scale. The balance came crashing down on the side of justice and the room erupted in applause and cheers!

The moment we had all been waiting for had finally arrived. And it came in a way none of us expected. As the pan came crashing down on the side of justice, the spirits of all who were there soared. Emboldened energy filled the room and in that moment the stature of nonviolence touched the sky. We beheld a powerful symbol of what it means to bring creativity and fresh energy to our vocation of peacemaking. And we were reminded that the presence of youth is an essential part of this work.

This story holds great lessons for us as we consider how to answer the call to rise in the contexts of our lives. It illustrates in a powerful way that each and every action for peace counts. Each stone placed on the scale symbolized an action taken by a person answering the call to rise. No matter how small an action may seem, none of them are insignificant. Each one brings us a little closer to tipping the balance of power toward justice. All of these actions together lead to the gradual transformation of our world. They tip the scale slowly and steadily toward justice. And we never know when our action may be the one needed to bring the balance crashing down on the side of justice.

Take a moment now to imagine these stones in a slightly different way. Each one of these stones is a building block of peace. We take an action for peace, and we place a building block alongside those placed by others. We seize a nonviolent moment, and we place another building block. Each one makes a unique and important contribution to the cultivation of peace in our world. And each one contributes to the growth of nonviolence as well. Some of these building blocks shore up the foundation for peace. Others raise the structure to ever greater heights. As the rows of these building blocks reach higher and higher, the stature of nonviolence steadily rises.

The climax in this story came when the young man placed his daughter on the balance. His strong desire to tip the scale motivated him to come up with something creative to make it happen. His example reminds us that there is ample room for creativity in answering the call to rise, and its role cannot be underestimated. New ideas and fresh approaches can raise the stature of nonviolence and hasten the day when the scales tip toward justice. Yet creative approaches can sometimes feel a little foolish to us. We must remember that Paul called his disciples to be fools for Christ. And being fools for Christ means we are fools for nonviolence, too.

This story reminds us that there is room for all of us to answer the call to rise. We can be like the father and call upon our creativity to inspire our work for nonviolence in new and exciting ways. We can also be like those who placed their stones on the balance in the way that was expected with no great fanfare. We do this by making our contributions to peace day by day, each of them a solid contribution to peacemaking and every one of them important. We can place our stones along the straight and narrow or we can scatter them in fresh designs and bold patterns of peace. Either way, we answer the call to rise and help nonviolence to ascend to greater heights in our society.

Finally, let me say a word about the important symbolism of the toddler who made all the difference in this story. Nonviolence is a lot like a toddler growing into the fullness of what it will one day be. It is filled with boundless energy and limitless possibilities to bring the world's balance crashing down on the side of justice. But like a small child, nonviolence needs to grow and develop in order to reach its full potential. Sometimes it will stumble and fall as it tries to find its way. And sometimes it will surprise us as it brings forth transformation in ways we never could have imagined.

We have seen examples of its stumbling and success both at home and abroad. Nonviolence rose up in nation after nation in the Middle East movement known as the Arab Spring, with varying degrees of success. It is rising up here at home with the growth of peace studies on college campuses and nonviolent conflict resolution in schools. Success and failure are both important to its growth, for it learns from its triumphs and its pitfalls in order to grow from the experience.

One important way we can tend to the growth of nonviolence is by mentoring those who are just beginning to explore or learn about the nonviolent way. We can share not only the lessons we have learned but also our passion for peace. We can share what we've come to know about nonviolence and its power to transform. And we can offer guidance on ways they can cultivate the spirituality of nonviolence in their own lives so that they have soul food to sustain them for the journey. In this way we enlighten others while also enlivening the vocation of peacemaking for a new generation. And we encourage nonviolence to reach for the stars upon the hopes and dreams of our youth.

Peacemakers who have entered their wisdom years have much to share with those who are just coming of age. I remember a gathering years ago that brought together Pax Christi elders and young adults. The elders included some of the organization's pillars like Eileen Egan and Bishop Tom Gumbleton. The gathering itself was a beautiful sight to behold and the conversations that took place were profound and prophetic. The wisdom of these elders was like fuel to the fire of unbridled enthusiasm burning in the hearts of the young adults. It was as if the torch of peace was being passed from those who had paved the pathway of peace to those who were just setting out on that same path.

What would it be like if the stature of nonviolence one day touched the skies? Society would finally recognize it as the legitimate tool of social transformation that it is. It would become a respected means of diplomacy in international relations. Nonviolence would be considered a top priority in resolving disputes at every level rather than a last-ditch effort. Fools for Christ would be respected as the founders of a new way of being. The way of nonviolence would become a way of life for more and more people. It would become the wellspring of community power in advancing social change. And it would lift a society deflated by retribution upon the breath of resurrection.

Nonviolence is capable of lifting our world to a way of life unlike anything we've ever known before. It can be the leaven that transforms unfriendly borders between nations into the building blocks of global community. Nonviolence can bring forth a world where God's one human family dwells with reverence for one another and for all creation. In this world, conflicts would be resolved not with weapons but with the wisdom of the nonviolent way. War would be a thing of the past and peace would be the way of the present.

It all begins when we answer the call to rise by standing tall in our nonviolent truths. So let us listen for this call in our lives and answer with courage and conviction each time it beckons. Let us rise up as fools creatively foiling the ways of violence as we forge the way of peace. Let us raise the stature of nonviolence remembering that we stand upon the shoulders of peacemakers who have gone before us. Let us rise upon the breath of resurrection that ascends to heaven from the depths of empty tombs.

When we join with others to answer the call to rise, we raise society to a better way of being. And we lift the stature of nonviolence toward heights that will one day reach beyond our wildest dreams.

Questions for Reflection and Conversation

1. What are the tombs brought about by violence that you have faced in your life? How have they called you to rise? And how have you answered?

2. How is nonviolence calling you to rise up at this point in your life? In what ways is it calling our world to rise up?

3. In what ways has our nation "nourished its anger" since September 11? In what ways have we nurtured our healing?

4. How do you live out your vocation of peacemaking? What does it require of you? What do you receive in return?

5. What is needed to raise the stature of nonviolence in society today? What is one thing you can do to help?

Conclusion

I READ SOMETHING AWHILE ago about the growth and development of nonviolence that caught my attention. I don't recall where I read it or who wrote it. But the article contained an important kernel of truth that I'd like to leave with you as you finish this book.

When we first encountered the word *nonviolence* years ago, the author noted, it was common to see it written as "non-violence." The hyphen played an important role in our understanding. It communicated clearly and simply that nonviolence is not violence. This mark of separation described nonviolence more in terms of what it isn't than what it is. It distinguished nonviolence as a force that is counter to violence and completely different from it. The author pointed out that it is now more common to see the word written as "nonviolence." By removing the hyphen, there is less emphasis on what it isn't and more emphasis on what it is.

This subtle shift in language reflects an important movement in real life. Nonviolence is growing and developing. It is coming into its own.

The author put into words something I've long felt. There is a sense of wholeness and integration that characterizes my understanding of nonviolence. I see the word written with a hyphen and without, and I used to wonder which version to use myself. But as I've grown in my understanding and practice of nonviolence, I've dropped the hyphen. Without it, the word takes on a sense of integration and wholeness. To embrace the spirituality of nonviolence is to recognize that all life is interwoven, and so our lived expression of it must be holistic. We share an innate connectedness through the web of life that binds us to one another and to all creation.

Living a life of nonviolence begins by striving to do no harm to people or the planet. And then it goes further. We come to understand that the strands in the web of life are all too easily broken. And so we work to reweave the web of life where it has been torn apart and tattered by violence.

The spirituality of nonviolence promotes healing in people and places broken by violence and cultivates reconciliation and right relationship. It calls us, in the spirit of Isaiah 58:12, to rebuild what has been ruined, repair what has been broken, and restore the streets we live in.

Nonviolence is and always will be a force to be reckoned with in countering violence in our world. But it is increasingly recognized as a force for reconciliation and healing as well. There is a great need to rebuild, repair, and restore what violence and injustice have ruined.

Over the years, there have been profound stories about reconciliation taking place in nations torn apart by violence and warfare. One of these is the story of South Africa. Once apartheid ended in this embittered nation, there was tremendous devastation left in its wake. There was no way to quickly or quietly wash away a gruesome legacy that had soaked this land in blood and scarred its conscience. Something different was needed to heal the country from its degrading and dehumanizing past.

The year was 1994 and Nelson Mandela had been elected the first democratic president. This man who was able to forgive his tormenters now governed a nation scarred by torment. So he sought to move the nation toward healing by following the path of reconciliation. The option of granting a blanket amnesty to the perpetrators of crimes was considered but rejected. The option of bringing the criminals to trial for gross human rights violations was also rejected for a variety of reasons. Finally, a third option emerged. South Africa would establish a Truth and Reconciliation Commission (TRC) that would allow the truth of the apartheid years to be told and the pain of these years to be released. In this way, it was hoped, the nation would move closer to reconciliation and healing.

The architects of this effort carefully created a process that brought before the TRC victims of the apartheid years as well as criminals longing to confess their crimes. The proceedings took place in hearings held all around the country. These hearings were open to the public, breaking the silence and secrecy surrounding the atrocities. It was decided that amnesty would be granted to those individuals who were willing to offer "a full disclosure relating to the crime for which amnesty was being sought."[1] Reparation of some sort would also be made available to victims. No one believed this process would be a perfect solution for cultivating healing in the heart of South Africa. But it offered a dignified way forward with a focus on repairing what had been broken and restoring the streets they lived in.

1. Tutu, *No Future Without Forgiveness*, 30.

As the people of South Africa went through this process, they recognized the importance of reconciliation for all involved. Healing was needed in the hearts of those who had been forced to carry out atrocities by their superiors. And healing was needed in the hearts of those who had endured these atrocities or lost loved ones to them. Criminals were granted an opportunity to openly confess the crimes they had committed and allow secrets tucked away in their souls to come forth. Victims and their loved ones were granted an opportunity to give voice to their experience and release their long-held anguish. The hearings became a forum for healing as those on both sides of the conflict were given a chance to speak their truth and listen to one another in a spirit of openness and honesty.

Bishop Desmond Tutu served as a valued member of the Truth and Reconciliation Commission and describes the experience in his book *No Future Without Forgiveness*. He writes that the testimony "made me realize that there is an awful depth of depravity to which we all could sink, that we possess an extraordinary capacity for evil. . . . [I]t is important to note that those guilty of these abuses were quite ordinary folk. . . . They looked just like you and me."[2] Bishop Tutu saw another side of the human condition as well. "It was the side that showed people who by rights should have been filled with bitterness because of the untold and unnecessary suffering they had endured. Instead, they were to demonstrate a remarkable generosity of spirit, an almost unprecedented magnanimity in their willingness to forgive those who had tormented them so."[3]

He then offers profound stories of courage, honesty, and forgiveness that took place during the hearings. One story speaks volumes about the desire for healing held deep within the heart of this battered nation. This hearing was held in Bisho, the site of the Bisho massacre that took place in September, 1992. Unarmed demonstrators had been marching for the right to free political activity when they were fired on by government forces. Thirty people died; twenty-nine who were marching for freedom and one government soldier. The hall was packed to overflowing on the day of the hearing. Many who were at the massacre, including those who were injured or lost loved ones, as well as government soldiers, were present. The room was filled with tension.

After several people spoke, an officer came forth and admitted that he, along with other officers in the government army, had given orders to the

2. Ibid., 144.

3. Ibid.

soldiers to open fire on the crowd that day. He then turned directly to the audience with a heartfelt plea for mercy. "I say we are sorry," he began. "I say the burden of the Bisho massacre will be on our shoulders for the rest of our lives. We cannot wish it away. It happened. But please, I ask specifically the victims not to forget. I cannot ask this, but to forgive us, to get the soldiers back into the community, to accept them fully, to try to understand also the pressure they were under then. This is all I can do. I'm sorry, this I can say, I'm sorry."[4]

The crowd, which had been filled with anger as the hearing began, broke into spontaneous applause. They had heard a confession that they desperately needed to hear. They were deeply moved by the honesty of the man. And in the face of such honesty, their hearts were moved to let go of their anger. Their applause affirmed the important step taken by this man in asking for forgiveness. And it affirmed their desire to forgive so that they might move beyond the darkness of the past toward the dawn of a new day. As I imagine the scene in the hall that day, I hear in the applause of the people the approval of our God, clapping right along with them and rejoicing in this movement toward healing and wholeness.

This powerful story highlights the yearning for reconciliation held deep in the hearts of so many who participated in the TRC hearings. Many of the criminals longed to be forgiven and many of those who had suffered injustice longed to forgive. Sometimes the victims lamented that they wanted to forgive but didn't know who to forgive since they didn't know who was responsible for the crime. In this case, one of those responsible had admitted his remorse and culpability. And those who were longing to forgive were given an opportunity to do so. "To work for reconciliation," writes Bishop Tutu, "is to want to realize God's dream for humanity—when we will know that we are indeed members of one family, bound together in a delicate network of interdependence."[5]

The process of reconciliation in South Africa offers an important example of how nonviolence is growing as people learn to bring its gifts to bear upon our world in new ways. It was a coordinated campaign of nonviolence at home and abroad that brought apartheid to its knees in South Africa. And it was a coordinated experiment in nonviolence that helped lift the soul of a nation toward healing. As the case of South Africa clearly demonstrates, nonviolence works to overcome injustice. And then it goes

4. Ibid., 150–51.

5. Ibid., 274.

further, working to heal the harm done at the hands of injustice. In this way it moves toward the fullness of nonviolence, with God acclaiming and affirming every step along the way.

We can see this movement in large-scale efforts like the process of reconciliation in South Africa. And we can see it in much smaller ways closer to home each time we foster reconciliation by entering into places broken by violence to ready the space for healing. "Each of us has a capacity for great good and that is what makes God say it was well worth the risk to bring us into existence," writes Bishop Tutu. "God . . . depends on us, puny, fragile, vulnerable as we may be, to accomplish God's purposes for good, for justice, for forgiveness and healing and wholeness."[6]

The more we do this, the more we expand the reach of nonviolence in our world. The more we grow into the fullness of nonviolence and allow its fullness to grow in us. And the more we experience the healing made possible at the hands of nonviolence.

When I began this book, I invited you to join me in taking off your shoes to honor the holy ground of the journey we were beginning. It's now time for you to put on your feet "whatever will make you ready to proclaim the gospel of peace" (Eph 6:15, NRSV). May you draw upon what you've discovered here as you go forth. The Scripture stories I've focused on are but a small sampling of all that Scripture has to offer you along the way. So much more is waiting to be discovered. I hope your eyes have been opened in ways that will help you behold the spirit of nonviolence stirring in other Scripture passages, inviting you to receive the wisdom that awaits you there.

As you go, keep in mind something I've learned along the way. Remember that our formation in the spirituality of nonviolence is ongoing. It does not end when we put down a book and pick up our walking sticks. It is not finished when we complete a course or a conference on peacemaking. Each of us is an ongoing act of creation. Just as nonviolence is growing in our world, so it will grow in us if we cultivate its growth. We foster the growth of nonviolence in our world by first fostering its growth in our lives. If we allow our own growth to become stagnant, we can expect our work for nonviolence will grow stale as well.

"When you are proclaiming peace with your lips," said St. Francis of Assisi, "be careful to have it even more fully in your heart."[7] These words are my prayer for you as you go forth. May you strive to proclaim peace

6. Ibid., 158–59.

7. St. Francis of Assisi, *Think Exist.*

not only with your lips but with your life as well. May you grow evermore fully in the way of nonviolence and may it grow in you. The more you give yourself to nonviolence, the more it will become a part of your being. The more it will flow from your life into the lives of those you touch. And the closer you will come toward realizing the fullness of nonviolence and the freedom it inspires.

Bibliography

Andreas, Joel. *Addicted to War: Why the U.S. Can't Kick Militarism*. Oakland: AK Press, 2004.

Brown, Raymond E., SS. *The Gospel According to John I–XII*. The Anchor Bible. New York: Doubleday, 1966.

Brueggemann, Walter, et al. *To Act Justly, Love Tenderly, Walk Humbly: An Agenda for Ministers*. Mahwah, NJ: Paulist, 1986.

Bush, George W. State of the Union Address. Washington, DC: January 29, 2002. White House archives. http://georgewbush-whitehouse.archives.gov/news/releases/2002/01/20020129-11.html.

Dickinson, Emily. *The Quote Garden*. www.quotegarden.com/sky-clouds.html.

Ellsberg, Robert, ed. *By Little and By Little: The Selected Writings of Dorothy Day*. New York: Albert A. Knopf, 1983.

Fellowship of Reconciliation. "Why is Colombia's the Most Under-reported War in the World?" *Witness*, Winter 2005, 5.

Ilibagiza, Immaculée, with Steve Erwin. *Left to Tell: Discovering God Amidst the Rwandan Holocaust*. Carlsbad, CA: Hay House, 2006.

The Interpreter's Dictionary of the Bible, K–Q. Nashville: Abingdon, 1962.

Kato, Shuson. In *Haiku Mind: 108 Poems to Cultivate Awareness and Open Your Heart*, by Patricia Donegan, 5. Boston: Shambhala, 2008.

King, Martin Luther, Jr. "Love in Action." In *Strength to Love*, 36–46. Philadelphia: Fortress, 1981.

———. "Loving Your Enemies." In *Strength to Love*, 47–55. Philadelphia: Fortress, 1981.

———. Speech at a victory rally following a favorable US Supreme Court decision desegregating Montgomery's buses, 1956. Women's International League for Peace and Freedom. http://wilpf.org/mlksbelovedcommunity.

Kownacki, Mary Lou. *Love Beyond Measure: A Spirituality of Nonviolence*. Erie, PA: Pax Christi USA, 1993.

Menchú, Rigoberta, and Elisabeth Burgos-Debray. *I, Rigoberta Menchú, An Indian Woman in Guatemala*. Translated by Ann Wright. New York: Verso, 1984.

National Conference of Catholic Bishops. *The Harvest of Justice is Sown in Peace: A Reflection on the Tenth Anniversary of The Challenge of Peace*. Washington, DC: November 17, 1993.

The National Priorities Project. *Military Spending in Fiscal Year 2013 and Beyond*. http://nationalpriorities.org/analysis/2012/presidents-budget-fy2013/military/.

———. *U.S. Security Spending Since 9/11*. http://nationalpriorities.org/analysis/2011/us-security-spending-since-911/.

New Revised Standard Version Bible. Anglicized ed. New York: Oxford University Press, 1989.

Pax Christi USA. *Peacemaking Day by Day*. Vol. 1. Erie, PA: Pax Christi USA, 1985.

———. *Peaceweavings*. Summer 2011. Washington, DC.

Pew Forum Poll. "Only A Minority of Americans Hold Favorable Views of Muslims." The Islamic Workplace. http://theislamicworkplace.com/2009/09/10/pew-forum-poll-only-a-minority-of-americans-hold-favorable-view-of-muslims/.

Pope Francis. "Address to the Faithful Gathered in St. Peter's Square." The Vatican: August 18, 2013. www.vatican.va.

Schaeffer-Duffy, Scott. "The Cross and the Sword." *The Catholic Radical*, August/September 2011, 1–2.

Schell, Jonathan. "The Unconquerable World." In *The Jonathan Schell Reader*, 387–432. New York: Nation, 2004.

St. Francis of Assisi. *Think Exist*. http://thinkexist.com/quotation/while_you_are_proclaiming_peace_with_your_lips-be/220425.html.

Svetlik, Jenn. "Passing the Peace." *Sojourners*, March 2010, 35–37.

The Inclusive Bible: The First Egalitarian Translation. Lanham, MD: Rowman and Littlefield, 2007.

The Water Project, Inc. *Why Water?* http://thewaterproject.org/why-water.php.

Tutu, Desmond. *No Future Without Forgiveness*. New York: Doubleday, 1999.

Tyler, Patrick E. "A New Power In the Streets." *New York Times*, February 17, 2003.

US Conference of Catholic Bishops. *Confronting a Culture of Violence: A Catholic Framework for Action*. Washington, DC: November, 1994.

Washington, James M., ed. *The Essential Writings and Speeches of Martin Luther King Jr*. New York: Harper Collins, 1991.

Wink, Walter. *Engaging the Powers: Discernment and Resistance in a World of Domination*. Minneapolis: Fortress, 1992.

Winter, Miriam Therese. *WomanWitness: A Feminist Lectionary and Psalter, Women of the Hebrew Scriptures: Part Two*. New York: Crossroad, 1992.

27108774R00095

Made in the USA
Middletown, DE
11 December 2015